2013 MOON BOOK
Living by The Light of The Moon

By Beatrex Quntanna

Acknowledgements

I wish to acknowledge: Stacey Sophia Robyn for making my dream to do another Moon Book a reality by painting the beautiful Moon Madonna called *Cyclic Dreaming*; Jennifer Masters for her sense of refinement and dedication to this project; Violet Lyall for her enthusiasm, teamwork, and endless nights editing; Michelenne Crab for her tech-support and personal support for the last 12 years; Nancy Ann Tappe, my mentor, for insisting I write this book every year for the last 16 years; Michael Makay for the numerology intentions for 365 days adding a new level of support to our calendar; Jill Estensen and Kaliani Devinne for contributing and calculating the Moon Charts. Special thanks to: Katherine Sale for the astrology calculations for the entire year. Last but not least, a deep gratitude to the countless students who come to Moon Class, without you guys this teaching would not exist.

Book Cover Art

Cyclic Dreaming
Stacey Sophia Robyn
staceyrobyn@gmail.com
www.StaceyRobyn.com

Book Design & Art Direction

Jennifer Masters
jennifer@new-temple.com

Copyright ©2012 by Beatrex Quntanna
All Rights Reserved. No part of this book may be reproduced or transmitted in any form or by any means without the written permission of the publisher, except for the inclusion of brief quotations in a review.

ISBN 978-0-9625292-2-1

Printed in the United States of America

ART ALA CARTE PUBLISHING
760-944-6020
beatrex@cox.net
www.beatrex.com

*This book is dedicated to Nancy Tappe,
a master-teacher and mystic who inspired
the creation of this book year after year.*

Table of Contents

The Importance of Cycles — 6

How to Use This Book — 7

January Calendar — 12
New Moon in Capricorn — 14
Full Moon in Leo — 22

February Calendar — 30
New Moon in Aquarius — 32
Full Moon in Virgo — 40

March Calendar — 48
New Moon in Pisces — 50
Full Moon in Libra — 58

April Calendar — 66
New Moon in Aries — 68
Full Moon in Scorpio — 76

May Calendar — 84
New Moon in Taurus — 86
Full Moon in Sagittarius — 94

June Calendar — 102
New Moon in Gemini — 104
Full Moon in Capricorn — 112

Table of Contents

July Calendar — 120
- New Moon in Cancer — 122
- Full Moon in Aquarius — 130

August Calendar — 138
- New Moon in Leo — 140
- Full Moon in Aquarius — 148

September Calendar — 156
- New Moon in Virgo — 158
- Full Moon in Pisces — 166

October Calendar — 174
- New Moon in Libra — 176
- Full Moon in Aries — 184

November Calendar — 192
- New Moon in Scorpio — 194
- Full Moon in Taurus — 202

December Calendar — 210
- New Moon in Sagittarius — 212
- Full Moon in Gemini — 220

About the Author — 229

The Importance of Cycles

Each moon cycle offers a different combination of energies. These energies pour down to the Earth, giving us a chance to grow harmoniously into wholeness. The key is to remember that this is a study in light. Following the luminaries, the Sun and the Moon, through the zodiac and noting the cycles of illumination and reflection can bring you to a deeper creative experience of life. The Moon is the great cosmic architect, the builder and dissolver of form and foundation. The Full Moon is about dissolving and the New Moon is about building. This workbook will assist you in knowing what to build and when, and what to dissolve and when.

The *2013 Moon Book* contains a valuable collection of knowledge developed by Beatrex over the years on how to use the moon cycles to enhance the quality of your life. It is a workbook filled with activities to do during each moon cycle, in its specific zodiac sign and time, for the entire year. Life, at the highest spiritual level, moves beyond time and uses cycles to increase your ability to actualize a full potential for living. Cycles are in charge of your personal development; while time is in charge of the change in direction that happens when you take the risk to grow and begin to trust in *divine timing*. This workbook synthesizes techniques that allow for the power of development and direction to occur in the entire spectrum of wholeness. Each zodiac sign holds the knowledge necessary to integrate an aspect of yourself in order to become whole. As the Moon and Sun travel around our planet each month, a different aspect of self-development is presented to you via the constellation (zodiac sign) it is visiting. For centuries, the Moon has been the keeper of the secrets of life. If used appropriately, the Moon sets the stage for successful living. This workbook reveals those secrets and supports you in learning them.

We are moving into a new paradigm for living that is now called The Fifth World, a time for *co-creation*. In order to co-create, we will be required to live in the moment, stay in our truth, accept what *is* without judgment, and live love. This will require adjustment and a re-calibration down to the core of our beings. It will also provide us with newfound freedom that requires us to give up our devotion to our past in order to embark on new frontiers. This year the workbook is set up with a support structure that easily guides you towards co-creation and freedom so that the power of acceptance can become your reality in 2013.

When the Moon is New

When the Moon is new, it is in the same sign as the Sun. This unites the power of the magnetic and dynamic fields that are in perfect resonance for co-creating. This is a potent time to make your desires known to yourself and to the Universe by writing a personal co-creation list. The dates and times are in your workbook as well as directions and ideas for the development of your co-creation list to actualize. The New Moon page in your book shows the astrological theme to be used in developing your list.

While considering the theme provided by the zodiac sign, write your list on the appropriate New Moon page in the workbook. Think about your list like a kid does when writing to Santa Claus. Let yourself become comfortable, while extending the boundaries beyond what you believe is possible. You might consider writing the following words at the end of your co-creation list, "This, or something better than this, comes to me in an easy and pleasurable way for the good of all concerned." Then, continue the co-creation process using the "Five Steps to Co-Creation" to assist you.

Once your list is written, light a candle, and read your list out loud. Then, place it under an eight-sided mirror, and put your candle on top of the mirror. Let the candle burn out. You might put the candle, wishes, and mirror outside in the moonlight or in a special place in your home. For your protection, make sure to use a candle that is in glass, such as a votive or 7-day candle. By the time the candle burns out, your co-creations are in place and ready to come true.

Note: It is best to do your creating and freedom ceremonies at the specific time noted. All times listed in the book are local to the Pacific time zone. Add or subtract hours accordingly to adjust times for your time zone.

When the Moon is Full

When the Moon is full, it is time to set yourself free. The Full Moon is the time when the Moon is in direct opposition to the Sun. This polarity provides a disintegrating effect that presents the best possible opportunity to dissolve anything that stands in the way of your personal freedom.

Several hours before a Full Moon you may experience a tension that happens when the Sun and Moon come into an oppossing position. This is an aspect that is asking you to learn to understand opposite natures without feeling the need to separate them. As a matter of fact, they are designed to teach you how to find the middle ground and integrate these opposites so that you cannot be manipulated by polarity. Integration creates unity which then creates harmony. The identifying polarity themes are provided for you on the appropriate Full Moon pages.

Write down how you would like to be free. Freedom ideas are provided in each Full Moon section of the book to help you make your list. Once you have written down your personal freedom list and read it out loud then light a candle. Place your freedom list under a circle mirror and put the candle on top of the mirror. You might put your list, mirror, and candle outside in the moonlight or in a special place in your home. For your protection, remember to use a candle that is in glass. When your candle has finished burning, your freedom list will be in operation. Remember that being free is as important as co-creating. It is the empty space that makes room for co-creation to occur.

Once you have written your freedom statements you may experience a limitation or two. If this happens, there is a special section called "Five Steps to Freedom" designed to assist you in finding your way out of any blocks.

Note: Mirrors are available at www.mymoonbook.com

how To Use This Book

These Sections Will Help You to Live by the Light of the Moon

Statements

These statements align the Self with the characteristics of the astrological sign and the house the sign lives in.

Body Mind Spirit

Each astrological sign rules a body part, a mental trait or attitude, and a spiritual condition. This section is provided to increase understanding of the tendencies and patterns that are activated during the moon transit.

List Ideas

Use these ideas to jump start your own lists. Let your imagination take off from here.

Gods and Goddesses

When the Moon enters a new zodiac sign, a changing of guardians occurs. Deep within each sign lives a God or Goddess who is the keeper of this cyclical domain. This archetype's assignment is to hold the space for an aspect of wholeness to actualize.

On Your Altar

An altar is an outer focus for inner work. Esoteric coordinates such as tarot cards, flowers, colors, gemstones, fragrance, and numerology are provided as an enhancement to better assist you in working with each moon phase. Perhaps you are working on a love theme; you might want to place six hearts, six flowers, and six gemstones along with your co-creation list and candle. The coordinating tarot card can be used as a visual activation. Flowers, colors, and gemstones accent your intentions. The fragrance provides a special connection to Spirit. You may want to burn candles of this scent, spritz your aura or your altar with the fragrance, or simply sniff the fragrance to awaken your olfactory system.

Note: Moon Mists are available at www.mymoonbook.com

Astrological Highlights

This section explains the planets and how they will affect your life each month. It does not contain all the aspects; it simply highlights points of interest that promote personal growth during each month. If you are interested in more study take an astrology class. If you are an astrologer and want more information we have provided a chart for each moon phase for your convenience.

Memory Maintenance Meditation

This section focuses on the freedom part of the moon cycle. The Moon governs our past history and the maintenance of our memory. It is our history that often creates blocks to achieving our goals. During the Full Moon phase, the Moon works with us to become free of past our history and converts it in to our memory where wisdom lives.

The Astro-Wheel

Western astrological charts are placed within a circle or wheel. The wheel is a picture of the sky from a particular place and time on Earth. It is divided into 12 parts called houses. Each house deals with a particular area of life. Key concepts for each house are written outside the wheel. Compare the wheel in the book to your very own chart and discover the theme that you will be living personally during the moon phase.

Cosmic Check-In

"I" statements are designed specifically to keep you in touch with all of the signs and their houses each time the Moon is new or full. Fill in the blanks to complete each statement during each full and new moon phase to activate all parts of your birth chart and keep you in touch with *Oneness*. Have fun noticing how different you are during each cycle.

Five Steps to Co-Creation

This demonstrates a method to use to play an active part in manifesting what it is that you want in your life.

Five Steps to Freedom

This section is a step-by-step approach to show you how to move beyond limits and become free.

Victories and Challenges

These are sets of affirmations designed to say out loud during a specific moon cycle to determine a motivational tone for your self-discovery. After saying all of them out loud, you will know which statement applies to you. Circle the one that is yours and use it as a personal mantra daily during the moon phase.

Questions to Ask Myself

These questions are assigned for each astrological sign. Filling them out will help you grow during each moon cycle.

The Monthly Calendar

This section provides you with a monthly overview and keeps you connected to the movements of the Sun, Moon, and planetary cycles. It lets you know when the Moon is void-of-course, when it moves into a new sign, when the Sun and planets change signs, and when a planet goes retrograde or stationary direct ($\frac{S}{D}$). As a special treat this year, the calendar has the Tibetan Numerology of the day at the bottom of each square of the grid along with a daily affirmation written by Michael Makay to align with the number and set your intentions for the day.

Tibetan Numerology of the Day

2	**Balance**	They ask us to be decisive and move past vacillation.
3	**Fun**	Have a party. Take on a creative project. Express the "Disneyland" side of yourself.
4	**Structure**	Take the day to organize. Get the job done. Work and you will sail through the day.
5	**Action, exercise, travel**	Join a gym. Take a dance class. Play tennis. Go for a drive. Make a change.
6	**Love**	Go out for a night of romance. Work on beauty in your home. Take care of your health.
7	**Research**	Read a book. Learn something new and get smart. Take a class.
8	**Money**	Have a business meeting. Meet with your accountant. Make a sales call. Start a new business.
9	**Connecting with the Divine**	Meditate. Take part in a humanitarian project. Do community service.
10	**Seeing the big picture**	Take an innovative idea and run with it today.
11	**Completion**	The finish line is available today.

Void Moon

When the Moon is void-of-course, it has made its last major aspect in a sign and stays void until it enters the next sign. When the Moon is void-of-course, you will see the icon V/C. This is not a good time to start new projects, relationships, or trips, unless you intend to never follow through. When the Moon ☽ enters a new sign, you will see this arrow ➡. It will be followed by the symbol for the new sign and the time the Moon enters it.

Super-Sensitivity ▲

This happens when the Moon travels across the sky and hits the center of the galaxy and connects with a fixed star. When this happens the atmosphere becomes chaotic. An extra amount of energy pours down in a spiral at a very fast speed making it difficult to focus. This fragility can make you depressed, anxious, dizzy, and accident prone. It is a good idea to keep your thought process away from this energy. It is global not personal.

Low-Vitality ▼

This happens when the Moon is directly opposite the center of the galaxy. When this fixed-star opposition occurs the Earth becomes very fragile and gets depleted. This leads to exhaustion in our physical bodies and is a sign for us to nurture ourselves by resting. This depletion can create Earth changes. Endings can also happen and resistance to these completions will bring on exhaustion. Best to detach and let go.

The Sun

Each month you will see the icon for the Sun ☉ with an arrow ➡ indicating when the Sun enters a new sign. When the Sun changes signs, the climate of energy takes on a new theme for your personal development. Look for the Sun icon with an arrow followed by an astrological sign to indicate sign change and time.

Planets

Planets also change signs and move in retrograde and direct motions. Retrograde planets are next to the date in each day's box followed by retrograde icon ℞. In the middle of each box is information about planetary changes of time and direction.

Please note: All times are given for the Pacific Time Zone. Add or subtract hours accordingly to adjust times for your time zone.

☉	Sun	Outer personality, potential, director, the most obvious traits of the consciousness projection
☽	Moon	Emotion, feelings, memory, unconsciousness, mother's influence, ancestors, home life
☿	Mercury	The way you think, the intention beneath your thoughts, communication, academia (lower mind)
♀	Venus	Beauty, value, romantic love, sensuality, creativity, social, fun, femininity
♂	Mars	Action, change, variety, sex drive, ambition, warrior, ego, athletics, masculinity
♃	Jupiter	Benevolent, jovial, excessive, expansive, optimistic, abundance, good fortune, extravagant
♄	Saturn	Teacher, karma, disciplined, restrictive, father's influence
♅	Uranus	Liberated, revolutionary, explosive, spontaneous, breakthrough, innovation, technology
♆	Neptune	Mystical, charming, sensitive, addictive, glamor, deceptive, illusions
♀ or ♇	Pluto	Money, wealth, transformation, secrets, hidden information, sexuality, psychic power
⚷	Chiron	Wounded healer, healing, holistic therapies
☊	North Node	Sometimes it is called the head of the dragon in Eastern Astrology. It represents where you are headed in this lifetime. In other words it represents the direction your life will take you, your future focus.
☋	South Node	Sometimes called the tail of the dragon in Eastern Astrology. It represents what you brought with you this lifetime and what you are moving away from.

Astrological Signs

Each sign of astrology has a particular quality or tone that is described in more detail with the moons.

Sign	"I" Statement		Element	Key Words
♈ Aries	I Am	Sign of the Ram Ruled by Mars ♂ Aries begins the zodiac year with the Spring Equinox	Fire	Ego, identity, championship, leadership, action-oriented, warrior, and self-first.
♉ Taurus	I Have	Sign of the Bull Ruled by Venus ♀	Earth	Self-value, abundant, aesthetic, business, sensuous, art, beauty, flowers, gardens, collector, and shopper.
♊ Gemini	I Communicate	Sign of the Twins Ruled by Mercury ☿	Air	Versatile, expressive, restless, travel-minded, short trips, flirt, gossip, nose for news, and messenger.
♋ Cancer	I Feel	Sign of the Crab Ruled by the Moon ☽ Cancer begins with the Summer Solstice	Water	Emotional, nurturing, family-oriented, home, mother, cooking, security-minded, ancestors, builder of form and foundation.
♌ Leo	I Love	Sign of the Lion and ruled by the Sun ☉	Fire	Willful, dramatic, loyal, children, child-ego state, love affairs, decadent, royal, show-stopper, theatre, adored and adoring.
♍ Virgo	I Heal	Sign of the Virgin Ruled by Mercury ☿	Earth	Gives birth to divinity, perfectionist, discernment, scientific, analytical, habitual, work-oriented, body maintenance, earth connection, attention to detail, service-oriented, earth healer, herbs, and judgmental.
♎ Libra	I Relate	Sign of the Scales Ruled by Venus ♀ Libra begins with the Autumnal Equinox	Air	Relationship, social, harmony, industry, the law, diplomacy, morality, beauty, strategist, logical, and over-active mind.
♏ Scorpio	I Transform	Sign of the Scorpion Ruled by Pluto ♀ and Mars ♂	Water	Intense, passionate, sexual, powerful, focused, controlling, deep, driven, and secretive.
♐ Sagittarius	I Seek	Sign of the Archer Ruled by Jupiter ♃	Fire	Optimistic, generous, preacher-teacher, world traveler, higher knowledge, goal oriented, philosophy, culture, publishing, extravagance, excessive, exaggerator, and good fortune.
♑ Capricorn	I Produce	Sign of the Goat Ruled by Saturn ♄ Capricorn begins at the Winter Solstice	Earth	Ambitious, concretive, responsible, achievement, business, corporate structure, world systems, and useful.
♒ Aquarius	I Know	Sign of the Water Bearer Ruled by Uranus ♅	Air	Inventive, idealistic, utopian, rebellion, innovative, technology, community, friends, synergy, group consciousness, science, magic, trendy, and future-orientation.
♓ Pisces	I Trust	Sign of the Fishes Ruled by Neptune ♆	Water	Sensitive, creative, empathetic, theatre, addiction, escape artist, glamor, secretive, divinely guided, healer, medicine.

The Astrology Wheel

Western astrological charts are placed within a circle or wheel. The wheel is a picture of the sky from a particular place and time on Earth. It is divided into 12 parts called houses. Each house deals with a particular area of life. Below are some key concepts for each house.

	Statement		Ruling Sign	Key Notes
1st House	I Am	♈	Aries	Your outer appearance, the way you present yourself, the way you dress, the way you enter a room, and what you leave behind when you leave the room.
2nd House	I Have	♉	Taurus	The way you make your money and the way you spend your money.
3rd House	I Communicate	♊	Gemini	How you get the word out and the message behind the words.
4th House	I Feel	♋	Cancer	The way your early environmental training was and how that set your foundation for living, and why you chose your mother.
5th House	I Love	♌	Leo	The way you love and how you want to be loved.
6th House	I Heal	♍	Virgo	The way you manage your body and its appearance.
7th House	I Relate	♎	Libra	One-on-one relationships, defines your people attraction, and how you work in relationships with the people you attract.
8th House	I Transform	♏	Scorpio	How you share money and other resources, what you keep hidden regarding sex, death, real estate, and regeneration.
9th House	I Seek	♐	Sagittarius	The way you approach spirituality, philosophy, journeys, higher knowledge, and aspiration.
10th House	I Produce	♑	Capricorn	Your approach to status, career, honor, and prestige, why you chose your Father.
11th House	I Know	♒	Aquarius	Your approach to friends, social consciousness, team-work, community service, and the future.
12th House	I Trust	♓	Pisces	Determines how you deal with your karma, unconscious software, and what you will experience in order to attain mastery by completing your karma. It is also about the way you connect to the divine.

Blank Pages

Between each moon phase we have provided blank pages for journaling.

January 2013

SUN	MON	TUE	WED	THU	FRI	SAT
		1 ♃℞ New Years Day ☽ → ♍ 9:36 AM 8. Abundance is your birthright.	**2** ♃℞ 9. Come from your heart.	**3** ♃℞ ☽ V/C 4:16 AM ☽ → ♎ 5:12 PM 10. A bright future starts now.	**4** ♃℞ 11. The Universe has no limits.	**5** ♃℞ ☽ V/C 3:14 PM ☽ → ♏ 10:10 PM 3. Joy is your choice.
6 ♃℞ Epiphany 4. Create your own structure.	**7** ♃℞ ☽ V/C 3:32 AM 5. Change is your friend.	**8** ♃℞▲ ☽ → ♐ 12:29 AM ☽ V/C 6:29 PM ♀ → ♑ 8:12 PM 6. Live and love every day.	**9** ♃℞▲ 7. Use an intelligent approach.	**10** ♃℞ ☽ → ♑ 12:55 AM 8. Money is meant to circulate.	**11** ♃℞ ● 21°♑46′ 11:45 AM ☽ V/C 11:45 AM 9. Develop a prayerful attitude.	**12** ♃℞ ☽ → ♒ 1:02 AM 10. Create a new beginning today.
13 ♃℞ ☽ V/C 12:38 AM 2.Stay in balance at all times.	**14** ♃℞ ☽ → ♓ 2:50 AM 3. A playful attitude helps.	**15** ♃℞ 4. Find the order that works for you.	**16** ♃℞ ☽ V/C 1:33 AM ☽ → ♈ 8:08 AM 5.Time for a play break.	**17** ♃℞ 6. Make family a priority.	**18** ♃℞ ☽ V/C 4:41 PM ☽ → ♉ 5:37 PM ☿ → ♒ 11:26 PM 7. Read a stimulating book.	**19** ♃℞ ☉ → ♒ 1:53 PM 8. Be in charge, not in control.
20 ♃℞ ☽ V/C 10:17 AM 9. Express your feelings carefully.	**21** ♃℞ Martin Luther King ☽ → ♊ 6:05 AM 10. An optimistic outlook wins.	**22** ♃℞▼ 11. Make everything work in your favor.	**23** ♃℞▼ ☽ V/C 3:43 AM ☽ → ♋ 7:01 PM 3. Structure belief based on experience.	**24** ♃℞ 4. Put your desk in order.	**25** ♃℞ ☽ V/C 12:36 PM 5. Do something in a different way.	**26** ♃℞ ○ 7°♌24′ 8:39 PM ☽ → ♌ 6:21 AM 6. Adorn your home with flowers.
27 ♃℞ 7. Learn something new and interesting.	**28** ♃℞ ☽ V/C 9:00 AM ☽ → ♍ 3:28 PM 8.Share what you have with others.	**29** ♃℞ 9. Be supportive to others in need.	**30** ♃S 6°♊19 3:38 AM ☽ V/C 6:00 PM ☽ → ♎ 10:37 PM 10. Think ahead to a fun vacation.	**31** 11. The Universe supports you always.		

January 2013 Planetary Highlights

Jupiter is retrograde in Gemini until the 30th of the Month

It's time to ask yourself where you were in 2001 regarding love, home, and health. Once you have located yourself in that time-frame, begin to remember the choices that you made at that time about those issues and make new choices. Because Jupiter is in Gemini it is very important to watch your words. The Law of Sound is in operation here and requires you to use your words wisely. Take time to "undo" anything that you have said that was not in your highest and best good or the best good for others in your life. This is a major time for using your thoughts and language to benefit your life. "Change your language, change your life" can have a very positive effect right now.

Neptune and Chiron are Conjunct in Pisces all Month

This coupling asks us to remember our interconnectedness with all and is the gateway to oneness on the planet. Healing through inner wisdom is the key here. We must accept the invitation that this conjunction provides by going deep to heal our inner Father. This begins our generational assignment to accept that a healing can occur in the hearts of all religions. Begin here by checking in to see what illusions and disappointments you might have around you own father.

January 8, 8:42 AM – Venus enters Capricorn

This is a time when romance meets Mr. Reasonable, which puts a damper on Venus and her creativity, sensuality, spontaneity, and spending habits. Resistance can lead to an uproar that will be very uncomfortable. It is best to see where a more practical approach might be necessary for a few weeks.

January 11 Moon-Sun-Mercury Conjunction in Capricorn

This is a directive to become aware of how you let your past bleed into today and spoil your thinking process by doing so. Stay in the present moment and keep your mind's attention on the present moment!

January 18, 11:26 PM – Mercury enters Aquarius

Prepare for an over-active mind to come forward. This can be an amazing time for mental brilliance to guide you toward an invention or a new frontier that will add to the quality of your life. Sudden impulses will guide you if vacillation doesn't take over. Put action to your thoughts and manifestation will occur. Go for it now!

January 8 and 9 – Super-Sensitivity ▲

Take it easy, the energy in the sky is connected to chaos and it is advisable to stay close to yourself. Avoid travel. Best not to meditate on these days.

January 22 and 23 – Low-Vitality ▼

Fragility is deep within the Earth today. Take it easy and rest.

♈ Aries	♋ Cancer	♐ Sagittarius	☽ Moon	♄ Saturn	☊ North Node	V/C Void-of-Course
♉ Taurus	♌ Leo	♑ Capricorn	☿ Mercury	♅ Uranus	☋ South Node	▲ Super-Sensitivity
♊ Gemini	♍ Virgo	♒ Aquarius	♀ Venus	♆ Neptune	→ Enters	▼ Low-Vitality
	♎ Libra	♓ Picses	♂ Mars	♀ or ♇ Pluto	℞ Retrograde	
	♏ Scorpio	☉ Sun	♃ Jupiter	⚷ Chiron	S/D Stationary Direct	

New Moon in Capricorn

January 11, 11:45 AM

Statement I Produce
Body Knees
Mind Tradition
Spirit Self-reliance

When the Sun is in Capricorn

The statement for the Capricorn is I Produce. It is important for all of us to feel useful and productive during this time. When the Sun is in this sign, we are given opportunities to receive the blessings of abundance and prosperity on a concrete level. Material satisfaction is at the top of the priority list for Capricorns. This is why they are known to be ambitious. Let integrity and goodwill set the standard for your recognition and accomplishments. Now is the time to take advantage of the energy by being useful and productive with a higher purpose. Capricorn is going through the most difficult times right now as the old guard is being swept away and creating space for the opening of the human heart. The presence of Pluto in this constellation is transforming all the systems and structures that are so familiar and placing the Capricorn on unstable ground. Authority symbols and traditions are dissolving and opening new pathways for self-reliance to emerge as a reality so that the idea of elitism can diminish and synergy will be the new status quo.

Capricorn God

Khronos is the God of Time. He is an incorporeal God who emerged formless at the beginning of Creation. In the beginning, he demonstrated this by creating himself as a snake with three heads: one a man, one a bull, and one a lion, all symbols of the primal world. Khronos is the consort to Anake, the Goddess of Inevitability. Together they circle the primal world weaving a tapestry of spirals that connect the Earth directly to the Ordered Universe, so that time can be birthed and everything will have an order to it. When the Moon is full in Capricorn, we must become free of our concern about time and learn to trust in the concept of inevitability by calling on the power of Khronos and Anake to know about timing.

Capricorn Co-Creation Ideas

Now is the time to focus on...

- Flexibility
- Productivity
- Authenticity
- Timing
- New Paradigms
- Transmuting
- Transformation
- Re-translating structure

On Your Altar

Colors: Forest green, tan, earth tones, deep red

Numerology: 9 – Connect with your purpose today

Tarot Card: The Devil – being a prisoner of a choice-less reality

Gemstones: Topaz, carnelian, amber, smoky quartz, jasper

Plant Remedy: Rosemary – the power of memory

Fragrance: Frankincense – opens the gateway for the Soul to enter the body

New Moon in Capricorn

January 11, 11:45 AM

Capricorn Challenges and Victories

Ultimate fulfillment is mine today! My willingness to live my life to the fullest each day is making all my dreams come true. I am fulfilling the promise of my destiny, and, in so doing, I make my mark on the world. I have completed my commitment to the Earth and to the cosmos by being all that I can be in the cycles of time on the inner and outer planes of awareness. All four seasons have been activated within me so that I am in alignment and in motion with the cycles of releasing, rebirthing, planting and harvesting.

I can now claim my citizenship in all four worlds. I am open and ready for the inspiration that the spirit world brings me. I am ready to conquer the mental world by using thought rather than thinking. I am open to the expression of my heart and the magnetic field of love that is ever-present in my experience. I am open to receiving abundance from Nature and I contribute to the physical world by actively manifesting my ideas into reality.

I am in harmony with the four elements and keep them active within me, as well as contribute to them externally. The element of air is within me as I breathe in the miracle of life. The element of earth is within me as I honor my body and use all its senses to enhance the quality of life. I honor the earth as my home and take complete stewardship of my home and property on this earth. I honor the water, the wellspring of life eternal, and allow for the flow of my feelings and emotions to be a creative influence in the unconscious and conscious planes. I honor the fire within me as the spark of light that is a source of inspiration in my experience, and in so doing I have fulfilled the promise of my destiny to live fully, freely and passionately on all levels and on all dimensions with my Earth-Cosmos connection.

Capricorn Homework

The Capricorn Moon is the reincarnation of Spirit emerging from the dark waters of our past emotions and releasing us from our fear of change and our fear of loss. Awaken your powerful and positive spiritual connection to be open to new possibilities. Ask yourself to move beyond your emotional loyalty to the past in order to co-create. We are reminded of our need for material and emotional security at this time. In order to insure this, we must learn to build a foundation for ourselves that is lit from within, made from the materials of love, goodwill, and intelligence. Give yourself permission to throw away your watch and celebrate living in the moment.

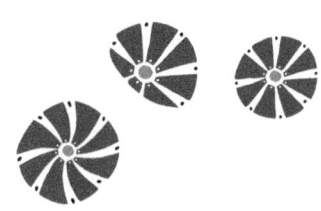

new Moon in Capricorn

January 11, 11:45 AM

Five Steps to Co-Creation

1. Acceptance

Acceptance opens the pathway to living in the moment and makes way for opportunity to occur. Co-creation can only occur when you live in the moment.

Start your list by writing… "I accept _____ into my life."

2. Adjustment

Consider what adjustments you may need to make in order to receive what you are accepting into your life.

My Co-Creation List

New Moon in Capricorn

January 11, 11:45 AM

3. Awakening

Once your list is complete, use the power of sound and read your list out loud. This directs your intentions (your list) toward actualization and co-creation.

4. Alignment

Now it is time to make a petition to the Universe, using these words, "I call on the power of the Universe to know I am ready to receive my list. I accept it. I allow it. So be it! This, or something better than this, comes to me in an easy and pleasurable way for the good of all concerned. Thank You Universe!" Light your candle and place it on your eight-sided mirror.

5. Acknowledgement

When a creation result is acknowledged it seals the deal. This makes room for more magnificence to expand into your life and increases your abundance factor adding to your ability to receive.

As each aspect of your co-creation list arrives in your life, spend time allowing, acknowledging, and accepting it with the true gusto of gratitude. You might want to make a victory list here.

Victory List

Capricorn Questions to ask Myself

How am I doing with transforming time into timing?

How can I transform my determination into inspiration?

If I was a father, what kind of father would I be to myself?

new Moon in Capricorn

January 11, 11:45 AM

How to Use the Moon Book With Your Chart

Fill in the blanks on the Cosmic Check-In page. Then look up the degree of the moon on the chart below. Take note of the "I" statement on the outside of the wheel where the moon is located. Now locate the same degree on your own chart, and make a note of the house and corresponding "I" statement. Go back to the Cosmic Check-In page and circle the two statements from the charts and read what you wrote. This will give you an idea about what to expect from this moon phase on a personal level.

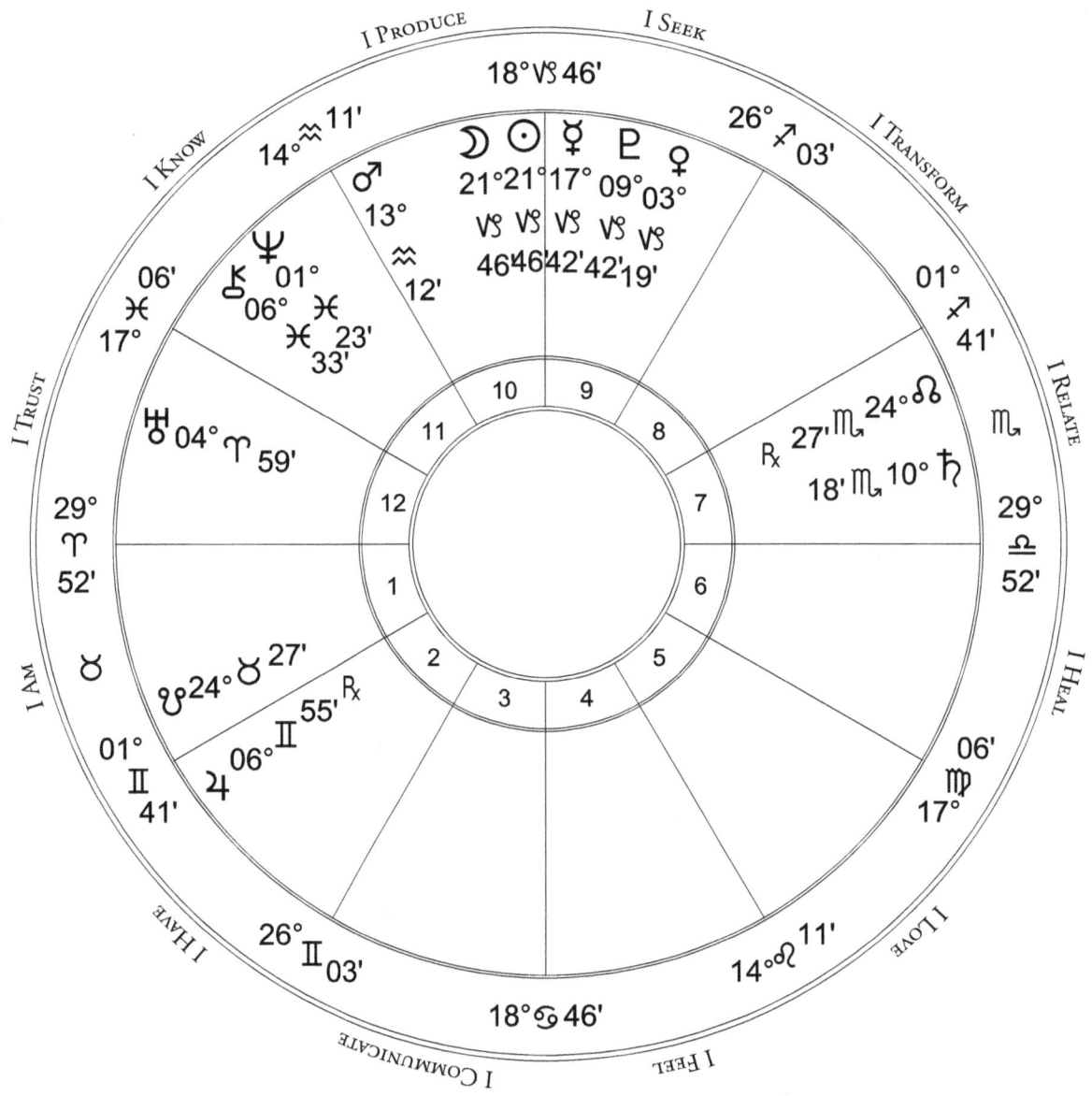

♈ Aries	♋ Cancer	♏ Scorpio	♓ Pisces	♀ Venus	♅ Uranus	☊ North Node
♉ Taurus	♌ Leo	♐ Sagittarius	☉ Sun	♂ Mars	♆ Neptune	☋ South Node
♊ Gemini	♍ Virgo	♑ Capricorn	☽ Moon	♃ Jupiter	♀ or ♇ Pluto	℞ Retrograde
	♎ Libra	♒ Aquarius	☿ Mercury	♄ Saturn	⚷ Chiron	

18

new Moon in Capricorn

January 11, 11:45 AM

Cosmic Check-In

Take a moment to write a brief phrase for each "I" statement.
This activates all areas of your life for this creative cycle.

♑ I Produce

♒ I Know

♓ I Trust

♈ I Am

♉ I Have

♊ I Communicate

♋ I Feel

♌ I Love

♍ I Heal

♎ I Relate

♏ I Transform

♐ I Seek

Full Moon in Leo

January 26, 8:39 PM

Statement I Love
Body Heart
Mind Self-confidence
Spirit Generosity

The Sun is Opposite the Moon

Full Moons are always in opposition to the Sun. This creates a feeling of tension between where you want to shine and how your feelings are flowing on a sensory level about the Sun's directive. The two forces seem like they are working against each other, yet they are on the same team displaying different techniques to attain the same mission. The Leo/Aquarius polarity creates tension about the need to be adored and the need to be free.

Leo God

Apollo, the God of Light, is gifted with extraordinary beauty and insight. Despite his magnificent beauty, he never experienced the true heart connection in love. He took the name of the sun god; however, he never performed his duties as such. He was personified as the ideal male, standing for order and reason. The gateway of his temple is inscribed with a statement, "Know Thyself." He attracted many adoring people because of his beauty, yet they never entered the realm of his heart. During the Full Moon in Leo, we must set ourselves free from the facets of emptiness that come from the desire to be adored rather than to be loved and loving.

Leo Freedom List Ideas

Now is the time to free myself from…

- The need to be the center of attention
- Obstacles to generosity
- False pride and false identity
- Blocks to confidence and creativity
- Excuses that keep me from quality time with my children
- Blocks to knowing I am loved and lovable
- The idea that everyone needs to be devoted to me in all situations

On Your Altar

Colors: Royal Purple, gold, orange

Numerology: 6 – Live Love Everyday

Tarot Card: Strength – passion for all of life

Gemstones: Amber, emerald, pyrite, citrine, yellow topaz

Plant remedy: Sunflower – standing tall in the center of life

Fragrance: Jasmine – remembering your Soul's original intention

Full Moon in Leo

January 26, 8:39 PM

Memory Maintenance Meditation

The Moon governs our memory and the maintenance of our memory. It is our memory that often creates blocks to setting us free to be able to attain our goals. The Moon works with us to help us become free from memory blocks three days after the Full Moon. The freedom themes are provided by the zodiac sign and can be from this lifetime or other lifetimes. These meditations assist in dissolving blocks and open pathways to new frontiers.

When the Moon is in Leo, we have the opportunity to see the records of our Soul's original intent. Close your eyes and take in a few deep breaths. Then, ask to make contact with an Angel of Records. Once that has been established, ask to be shown a time when you lost your original intent and replaced it with self-appointed authority. Honesty is the key to the Leo Moon. Ask for help to set yourself free from the self-appointed authority and accept the grace that re-connects to your original intention. The Leo Full Moon connects solar power to your power, and the angel brings a refreshment of grace.

Leo Challenges and Victories

I no longer feel the need to be in control and dominated by my mind telling me that it is appropriate to repress my feelings. I am going to claim my dominion today and feel the power of life running through me. I accept the privilege of being fully human and fully alive. I look to see where I lack courage to connect to what is natural for me. I see where I have been stubborn and turn to face my resistance. I become aware where my higher self says "Go" and my lower self says "No."

I am aware that my lower self (my Body) is a creature of habit and will sabotage me with the idea that change takes too much energy. I take responsibility for the part of me that is a creature of habit and talk to my body about coming into alignment with my new intention to become fully passionate and fully alive. I remember today that in order to get the body to move forward with me, I need two thirds of my cells to align with my request.

First, I become aware of the part of myself that is trying to control all of my outcomes and keep me a slave to those outcomes rather than trusting in the evolution of nature and the concept of Divine Order. I give up the fight today knowing that this struggle is dissipating all my energy and making me exhausted. In order for my body to respond, I need to awaken my cells through sound and touch. So today, I rub my body and speak out loud by sharing my request for connection, revitalization, rejuvenation, passion, and support. Today, I celebrate the idea that I can connect to my wholeness by activating my cells to support my commitment to my aliveness. I can now stand tall in the center of life and grow in Self-Confidence.

Leo Homework

Review your memorabilia and see what no longer matches your current love nature, your creative nature, and your loving self. Set your heart free while chanting, "Love is all you need." Become a part of the new consciousness on the Earth that brings a more abundant life when we expand the radius of our love. Live Love Every Day!

Full Moon in Leo

January 26, 8:39 PM

Five Steps to Freedom

When we work with the concept of freedom we are soon presented with resistance. Freedom presents a pathway for us to bump directly into our limitations. When we can become aware of these limits, we can then find our way to freedom. Below are some ideas that might assist you in seeing deeper into your resistance to accepting freedom into your life. Once you discover these you might want to add more to your freedom list.

1. Feeling Useless

This happens when you measure yourself by what others think of you.

2. Discouragement

This occurs when you use blame others instead of taking responsibility for your part in a situation.

3. Regret

This happens when you live inside past events and continue to rehearse your story, hoping that if you tell it enough, it will get resolved. Living in the past leads to regret and blocks you from freedom.

4. Limitation

This happens when we think that there is no way out of a challenge, which creates an inability to see options. When options are out of the picture we become unable to create positive outcomes.

5. Self-Doubt

This takes place when we think that others are better than we are. Growing cannot occur when we have given someone else our ceiling.

Full Moon in Leo

January 26, 8:39 PM

My Freedom List

Leo Questions to Ask Myself

How can I align with the integrity of my Soul?

How is the rhythm of my heart seeking expression in my body?

If I were a king how would I rule my Kingdom?

full Moon in Leo

January 26, 8:39 PM

How to Use the Moon Book With Your Chart

Fill in the blanks on the Cosmic Check-In page. Then look up the degree of the moon on the chart below. Take note of the "I" statement on the outside of the wheel where the moon is located. Now locate the same degree on your own chart, and make a note of the house and corresponding "I" statement. Go back to the Cosmic Check-In page and circle the two statements from the charts and read what you wrote. This will give you an idea about what to expect from this moon phase on a personal level.

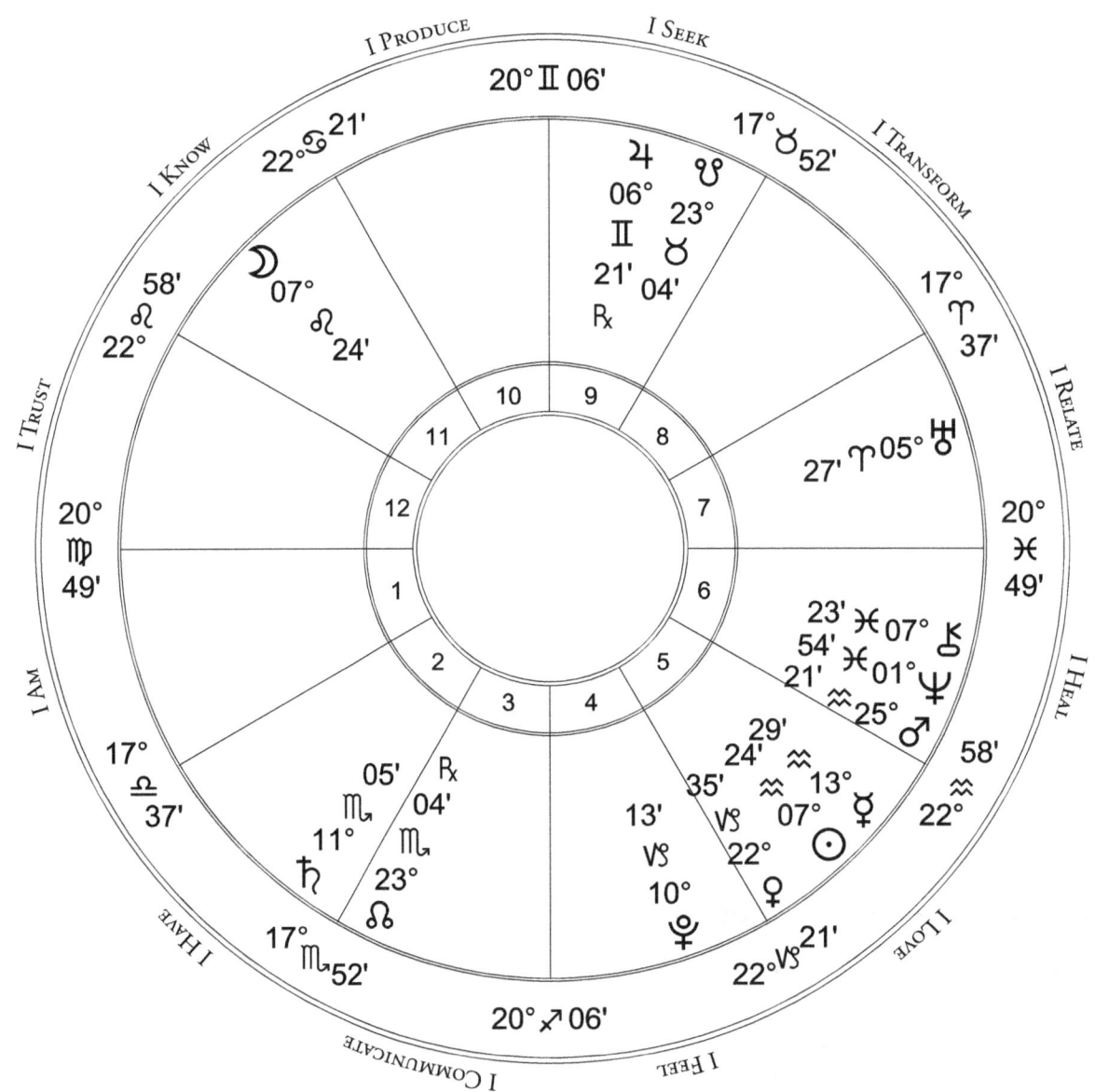

♈ Aries	♋ Cancer	♏ Scorpio	♓ Pisces	♀ Venus	♅ Uranus	☊ North Node
♉ Taurus	♌ Leo	♐ Sagittarius	☉ Sun	♂ Mars	♆ Neptune	☋ South Node
♊ Gemini	♍ Virgo	♑ Capricorn	☽ Moon	♃ Jupiter	♀ or ♇ Pluto	℞ Retrograde
	♎ Libra	♒ Aquarius	☿ Mercury	♄ Saturn	⚷ Chiron	

full Moon in Leo

January 26, 8:39 PM

Cosmic Check-In

Take a moment to write a brief phrase for each "I" statement.
This activates all areas of your life for this freedom cycle.

♌ I Love

♍ I Heal

♎ I Relate

♏ I Transform

♐ I Seek

♑ I Produce

♒ I Know

♓ I Trust

♈ I Am

♉ I Have

♊ I Communicate

♋ I Feel

February 2013

SUN	MON	TUE	WED	THU	FRI	SAT
				1 ☽ V/C 5:04 PM ♂ → ♓ 5:55 PM ♀ → ♒ 6:48 PM 3. Making money can be fun.	**2** Groundhog Day ☽ → ♏ 4:03 AM 4. Simplicity is the best organizer.
3 5. Be willing to change.	**4** ☽ V/C 4:32 AM ☽ → ♐ 7:46 AM 6. Review your health profile.	**5**▲ ♀ → ♓ 6:56 AM ☽ V/C 12:43 PM 7. Your every word has power.	**6**▲ ☽ → ♑ 9:56 AM 8. Be a leader without followers.	**7** ☽ V/C 4:45 AM 9. Be a good listener.	**8** ☽ → ♒ 11:17 AM 10. Surround yourself with beauty.	**9** ● 21°♒43' 11:21 PM Chinese New Year Enter the Snake ☽ V/C 11:21 PM 11. Above all else, be yourself.
10 ☽ → ♓ 1:21 PM 3. Be sure your beliefs are your own.	**11** ☽ V/C 9:04 AM 4. If it is logical, it will work.	**12** Mardi Gras ☽ → ♈ 5:52 PM 5. Match your energy to the situation.	**13** Ash Wednesday 6. Does your home reflect who you are?	**14** Valentine's Day ☽ V/C 7:36 PM 7. The power of the mind can heal.	**15** ☽ → ♉ 2:09 AM 8. Make money make a difference.	**16** 9. Be available to someone in need.
17 ☽ V/C 12:32 PM ☽ → ♊ 1:51 PM 10. Be open to a new beginning.	**18** ♄ᴿ President's Day ♄ᴿ–11°♏31' 9:03 AM ☉ → ♓ 4:03 AM 11. Allow your creativity to soar.	**19** ♄ᴿ▼ ☽ V/C 10:49 AM 3. Learn something from a child today.	**20** ♄ᴿ▼ ☽ → ♋ 2:46 AM 4. Move in a logical progression.	**21** ♄ᴿ ☽ V/C 6:09 PM 5. A change of pace is a good idea.	**22** ♄ᴿ ☽ → ♌ 2:13 PM 6. Live from your heart today.	**23** ♀♄ᴿ ♀ᴿ–19°♓52' 1:42 AM 7. Be open to doing research.
24 ♀♄ᴿ Purim ☽ V/C 8:51 PM ☽ → ♍ 10:53 PM 8. There is plenty for everyone.	**25** ♀♄ᴿ 7°♍24' 12:26 PM ♀ → ♓ 6:04 PM 9. Listen to what Spirit has to say.	**26** ♀♄ᴿ ☽ V/C 10:14 AM 10. Be willing to start anew.	**27** ♀♄ᴿ ☽ → ♎ 5:03 AM 11. Imagination is a wonderful tool.	**28** ♀♄ᴿ ☽ V/C 12:38 AM 3. Create your own belief system.		

February 2013 Planetary Highlights

February 1, 5:55 PM – Mars enters Pisces

Expect some steam to wave through the deep parts of your emotional body. Use this steam to awaken parts of yourself that need cleansing and all will be well. Resistance could lead to the need for an escape drama however that plays out.

February 1, 6:48 PM – Venus enters Aquarius

This presents an awakening in the creative aspect of the mind and, if used correctly, can become very valuable for a project that is coming forward. It will also bring about a more detached process where love issues are concerned; giving you a chance to observe what is really happening without the emotional charge.

February 5, 6:57 AM – Mercury enters Pisces

Give voice to your feelings. Set up times for meditation to hear what divinity is telling you.

February 9 – Chinese New Year: Enter the Water Snake

Ancient Chinese wisdom says a snake in the house is a good omen because it means that your family will not starve. People born in the Year of the Snake are keen and cunning, quite intelligent, beautiful, charming, and wise. They are great mediators and good at doing business. Snake years are about good fortune in business.

February 9 – Mars-Neptune Coupled in Pisces

Rose-colored glasses and impulsive action could lead to a disappointment. Use great caution dealing with drugs and please practice safe sex.

February 9 – Mercury-Chiron Conjunct in Pisces

Communication is up to bat for healing. Pay attention to your mind questioning all of your communications. Did I say too much? Or, did I hide by not saying enough? It's time to tell the truth and heal.

February 18, 9:04 AM – Saturn goes Retrograde in Scorpio

The body will let you know what it needs for healing, maintenance, and recalibration. Pay attention! The grand teacher is in there for a reason. Seek authorities in the healing arts, if necessary. Now is the time to nurture your body!

February 18, 4:03 PM – Sun enters Pisces

Divinity comes into action. It's time to trust what your intuition is telling you.

February 23, 1:42 AM – Mercury goes Retrograde

Avoid travel if possible. It's time to review old business and refrain from making any commitments in new business. Think twice before speaking.

February 25, 9:04 AM – Venus enters Pisces

Romance is in the air. Let love fill your soul. Live Love Every Day!

February 25 – Sun-Neptune-Chiron Tripled in Pisces

The directive here is to discover where you have identified what needs to heal in your heart as it relates to your experience of Divinity.

February 25 – Mars and Mercury Retrograde Conjunct in Pisces

This is a trigger-fest for the mind and ego as they try to determine who is "top dog." The battlefield of the mind tries to stay afloat on the steamy waves of Pisces.

February 25 – Moon Opposing Chiron, Sun, Neptune in Pisces

This could be a major slideshow of past life experiences. Meditate and update yourself by remembering it is 2013.

February 5-6 – Super-Sensitivity ▲

The atmosphere is chaotic keep your mind close by to avoid toxic thinking.

February 19-20 – Low-Vitality ▼

The Earth is fragile now so take extra care of your body.

♈ Aries	♋ Cancer	♐ Sagittarius	☽ Moon	♄ Saturn	☊ North Node	V/C Void-of-Course
♉ Taurus	♌ Leo	♑ Capricorn	☿ Mercury	♅ Uranus	☋ South Node	▲ Super-Sensitivity
♊ Gemini	♍ Virgo	♒ Aquarius	♀ Venus	♆ Neptune	➡ Enters	▼ Low-Vitality
	♎ Libra	♓ Picses	♂ Mars	♀ or ♇ Pluto	℞ Retrograde	
	♏ Scorpio	☉ Sun	♃ Jupiter	⚷ Chiron	S/D Stationary Direct	

New Moon in Aquarius

February 9, 11:21 PM — Chinese New Year: Enter the Water Snake

Statement I Know
Body Ankles
Mind True genius
Spirit Vision

When the Sun is in Aquarius

This is a time when the higher octave of the mind comes into play and one is given the power of vision. The Aquarian energies promote knowing by being a wellspring of knowledge. They expand the radius of contact by going beyond the known in areas of communication and cooperation. Now is the time to be initiated into greater awareness to serve the fields of human endeavors. Connect and combine magic with science and become a creative influence.

Aquarius Co-Creation Ideas

Now is the time to focus on...

- Vision
- Invention
- Technology
- Freedom
- Friends
- Community
- Personal genius
- Higher Awareness
- Team work
- Science and Magic

Aquarian Goddess

The Aquarian goddess, Star Woman, is also known as Hathor, the keeper of the light who gives birth to insight. All goddesses are born from the stars. Star Woman is in charge of directing the light bodies through the void of Creation to the point of insight, which occurs when the radiance is instilled in the memory of creation. She instills the light of the world into your own being so you can become in service to the souls who have lost their way.

On Your Altar

Colors: Violet, neon, crystalline rainbow tints

Numerology: 11 – Connecting to the vastness of the Universe

Tarot Card: The Star – golden opportunities for the future

Gemstones: Aquamarine, blue topaz, peacock pearls

Plant Remedy: Queen of the Night Cactus – ability to see light in the dark

Fragrance: Myrrh – healing the nervous system

new Moon in Aquarius

February 9, 11:21 PM — Chinese New Year: Enter the Water Snake

Aquarius Challenges and Victories

Today I chart my course for my new direction. My future is set on a new, fresh evolutionary course. I am guided by a higher source and trust in that guidance. I know my life has value and I am willing to contribute to the pool of consciousness by experiencing my life and living my life to the fullest view of possibility. Today I know my possibilities are endless. My Spirit and my Soul are connected to heaven and to earth and this knowing brings me to the awareness that I can add to the higher qualities of life because I am connected to the whole. My being is far reaching and immeasurable. I contribute to existence simply by knowing. All the guideposts are connected today for me to see my way to a profound new future. My vision is clear and I can clearly set my sights on this new course.

Golden opportunities come with this new vision and I trust in my guidance to bring me to this new level of manifesting power. I check in with my inner lights each day by meditating and asking for all seven of the energy centers in my body to come into alignment with the outer symbols of guidance. I do this by becoming still and breathing until I feel the stillness. Then, I place my hand on each center in the body, one center at a time, to be activated by light. Next, I ask out loud for each center in my body to let me know what its energetic contribution to the new direction is and how best to use the energy of the center to move forward on my new course of action. I write down each statement and connect each statement to the guiding star in the sky. I am now linked up physically and spiritually and totally ready to navigate my total self towards my new evolutionary direction.

Aquarian Homework

Aquarians co-create a store house of information through innovative telecommunications, technology, social networking and media, and global communication. They are typically found in the fields of psychology, science fiction authoring or film making, speech writing, and aerospace engineering.

Consider these three Aquarian gifts:

- Opportunity – become a creative influence
- Enlightenment – when you become aware that you are light
- Brotherhood – separation doesn't exist anymore

Where do you see these occurring in your life?

New Moon in Aquarius

February 9, 11:21 PM — Chinese New Year: Enter the Water Snake

Five Steps to Co-Creation

1. Acceptance

Acceptance opens the pathway to living in the moment and makes way for opportunity to occur. Co-creation can only occur when you live in the moment.

Start your list by writing… "I accept _____ into my life."

2. Adjustment

Consider what adjustments you may need to make in order to receive what you are accepting into your life.

My Co-Creation List

new Moon in Aquarius

February 9, 11:21 PM — Chinese New Year: Enter the Water Snake

3. Awakening

Once your list is complete, use the power of sound and read your list out loud. This directs your intentions (your list) toward actualization and co-creation.

4. Alignment

Now it is time to make a petition to the Universe, using these words, "I call on the power of the Universe to know I am ready to receive my list. I accept it. I allow it. So be it! This, or something better than this, comes to me in an easy and pleasurable way for the good of all concerned. Thank You Universe!" Light your candle and place it on your eight-sided mirror.

5. Acknowledgement

When a creation result is acknowledged it seals the deal. This makes room for more magnificence to expand into your life and increases your abundance factor adding to your ability to receive.

As each aspect of your co-creation list arrives in your life, spend time allowing, acknowledging, and accepting it with the true gusto of gratitude. You might want to make a victory list here.

Victory List

Aquarian Questions to ask Myself

How can I be a creative influence?

What flashes of genius are coming to me with a new point of view?

What re-wiring am I feeling in my nervous system that is guiding me to higher awareness?

new Moon in Aquarius

February 9, 11:21 PM — Chinese New Year: Enter the Water Snake

How to Use the Moon Book With Your Chart

Fill in the blanks on the Cosmic Check-In page. Then look up the degree of the moon on the chart below. Take note of the "I" statement on the outside of the wheel where the moon is located. Now locate the same degree on your own chart, and make a note of the house and corresponding "I" statement. Go back to the Cosmic Check-In page and circle the two statements from the charts and read what you wrote. This will give you an idea about what to expect from this moon phase on a personal level.

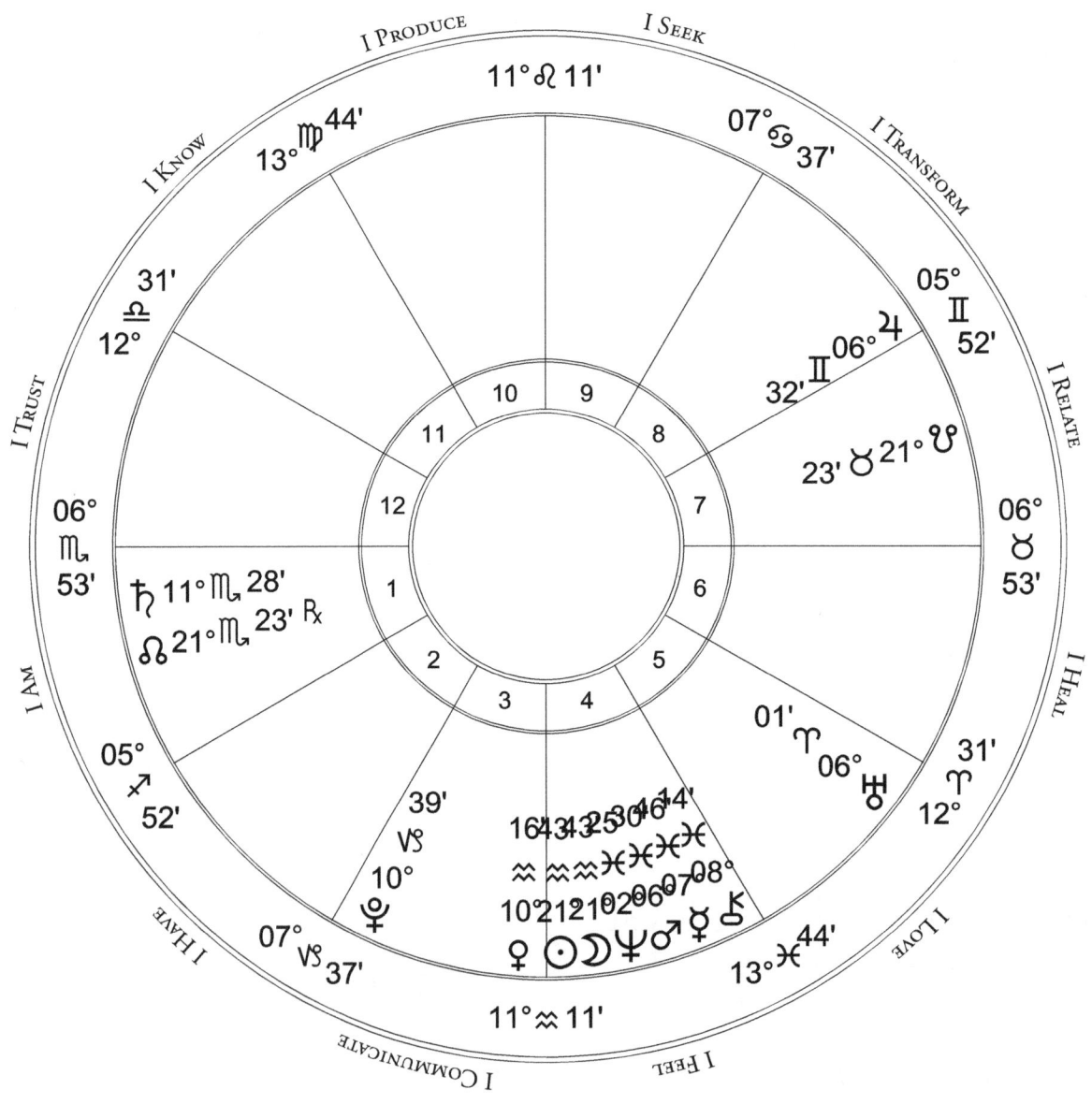

♈ Aries	♋ Cancer	♏ Scorpio	♓ Pisces	♀ Venus	♅ Uranus	☊ North Node
♉ Taurus	♌ Leo	♐ Sagittarius	☉ Sun	♂ Mars	♆ Neptune	☋ South Node
♊ Gemini	♍ Virgo	♑ Capricorn	☽ Moon	♃ Jupiter	♀ or ♇ Pluto	℞ Retrograde
	♎ Libra	♒ Aquarius	☿ Mercury	♄ Saturn	⚷ Chiron	

New Moon in Aquarius

February 9, 11:21 PM — Chinese New Year: Enter the Water Snake

Cosmic Check-In

Take a moment to write a brief phrase for each "I" statement.
This activates all areas of your life for this creative cycle.

♒ I Know

♓ I Trust

♈ I Am

♉ I Have

♊ I Communicate

♋ I Feel

♌ I Love

♍ I Heal

♎ I Relate

♏ I Transform

♐ I Seek

♑ I Produce

Full Moon in Virgo

February 25, 12:26 PM

Statement I Heal
Body Intestines
Mind Analytical
Spirit Discernment

The Sun is Opposite the Moon

Full Moons are always in opposition to the Sun. This creates a feeling of tension between where you want to shine and how your feelings are flowing on a sensory level about the Sun's directive. The two forces seem like they are working against each other, yet they are on the same team displaying different techniques to attain the same mission. The Virgo/Pisces polarity creates tension between doing your work and the need to find your path.

Virgo Goddess

Gaia gave birth to herself out of Chaos. After her own birth, she immediately gave birth to Uranus, the King of the Universe. Gaia is the creator of Heaven and Earth. She is the symbol for all that is natural, unlike her counterpart Uranus, who rules the Sky. She rules the womb and enclosed spaces. She is the Earth, giving birth to all of life and all organisms that shape the Earth's biosphere. When the Moon is full in Virgo, we are given the opportunity to look at what we have birthed within ourselves and set ourselves free from what is no longer giving us energy. Virgo sees Divinity in the details, so take a close look at what needs to be released to restore your physical energy.

Virgo Freedom List Ideas

Now is the time to free myself from...

- Finding fault with myself
- My addiction to perfection
- My addiction to detail
- Over-indulging in image management
- Pain-producing thinking patterns
- Judgment of others
- Resistance to being healthy
- Destructive behaviors

On Your Altar

Colors: Green, blue, earth tones

Numerology: 9 – listen to what Spirit has to say

Tarot Card: The Hermit – knowing your purpose and sharing it with the world

Gemstones: Emerald, sapphire

Plant Remedy: Sage – the ability to hold and store light

Fragrance: Lavender – management and storage of energy

Full Moon in Virgo

February 25, 12:26 PM

Memory Maintenance Meditation

The Moon governs our memory and the maintenance of our memory. It is our memory that often creates blocks to setting us free to be able to attain our goals. The Moon works with us to help us become free from memory blocks three days after the Full Moon. The freedom themes are provided by the zodiac sign and can be from this lifetime or other lifetimes. These meditations assist in dissolving blocks and open pathways to new frontiers.

When the Moon is in Virgo, the nighttime is sleepless and restless due to mental anxiety coming face-to-face with the thought world. Sit quietly and close your eyes. Breathe in and breathe out. It is a time to discover truth through action, and to detach from pain-producing thinking patterns which lead us to addiction. Ask for an Angel of Records to take you to a moment in time when you chose self-destructive behavior to mask anxiety. Release the addictive thinking patterns that control you. Ask for help from the Angel to see a way to accept the depth of your feelings.

Virgo Challenges and Victories

Today I take time to go within to be silent. I imagine myself on a country road moving towards a beautiful mountain. I bask in the glory of the power of the mountain and know that it is calling me to the top. I find a pathway to the top and begin to climb. While I am climbing I become aware of a presence guiding me and empowering me to keep going.

I find a sense of peacefulness in me with this presence. I become aware of my own power in this silent journey to the top and revel in the peacefulness that nature and silence bring me. At last I am about to reach the summit and, just before I do, I feel the power drawing me to go within on a deeper level. I stop for a moment and look back at the path I have just climbed and know that my life's path is a remarkable gift. I connect to the center of the Earth and feel an inner glow.

The top of the mountain calls to me and, as I reach the top, a voice says to me, "Take in the view and look in all directions." I do my 360° turn and, as I do, I sense a light igniting me in every direction. Then the voice says, "Look up!" Now, my awareness shifts and I see that I have become an illuminating light glowing in all six directions. Then the voice says, "Sit in your silence and take in the vastness of who you are. Who you are is immeasurable." I sit, feeling the glow of light within me, and become aware of a greater plan for my life. I allow myself to receive this plan. I accept this assignment and slowly walk down the mountain knowing that I can be a shining light for myself and others. I know I must take my light out to the world and share what I know to be my truth. Today, I become a messenger for the light.

Virgo Homework

Become integrated so that the light of your personality becomes soul-infused. When we are soul-infused and are in service to our higher self, we radiate love and light through the power of the inner self through all activities, thoughts, and emotions and become more magnificent. Learn the art of detachment and let your soul take control.

full Moon in Virgo

February 25, 12:26 PM

Five Steps to Freedom

When we work with the concept of freedom we are soon presented with resistance. Freedom presents a pathway for us to bump directly into our limitations. When we can become aware of these limits, we can then find our way to freedom. Below are some ideas that might assist you in seeing deeper into your resistance to accepting freedom into your life. Once you discover these you might want to add more to your freedom list.

1. Feeling Useless

This happens when you measure yourself by what others think of you.

2. Discouragement

This occurs when you use blame others instead of taking responsibility for your part in a situation.

3. Regret

This happens when you live inside past events and continue to rehearse your story, hoping that if you tell it enough, it will get resolved. Living in the past leads to regret and blocks you from freedom.

4. Limitation

This happens when we think that there is no way out of a challenge, which creates an inability to see options. When options are out of the picture we become unable to create positive outcomes.

5. Self-Doubt

This takes place when we think that others are better than we are. Growing cannot occur when we have given someone else our ceiling.

Full Moon in Virgo

February 25, 12:26 PM

My Freedom List

Virgo Questions to Ask Myself

How can I train myself to see the best in people?

How can I be a sentinel for harmonized awareness?

What is the best way for me to raise my vibration and remain connected to the earth?

full Moon in Virgo

February 25, 12:26 PM

How to Use the Moon Book With Your Chart

Fill in the blanks on the Cosmic Check-In page. Then look up the degree of the moon on the chart below. Take note of the "I" statement on the outside of the wheel where the moon is located. Now locate the same degree on your own chart, and make a note of the house and corresponding "I" statement. Go back to the Cosmic Check-In page and circle the two statements from the charts and read what you wrote. This will give you an idea about what to expect from this moon phase on a personal level.

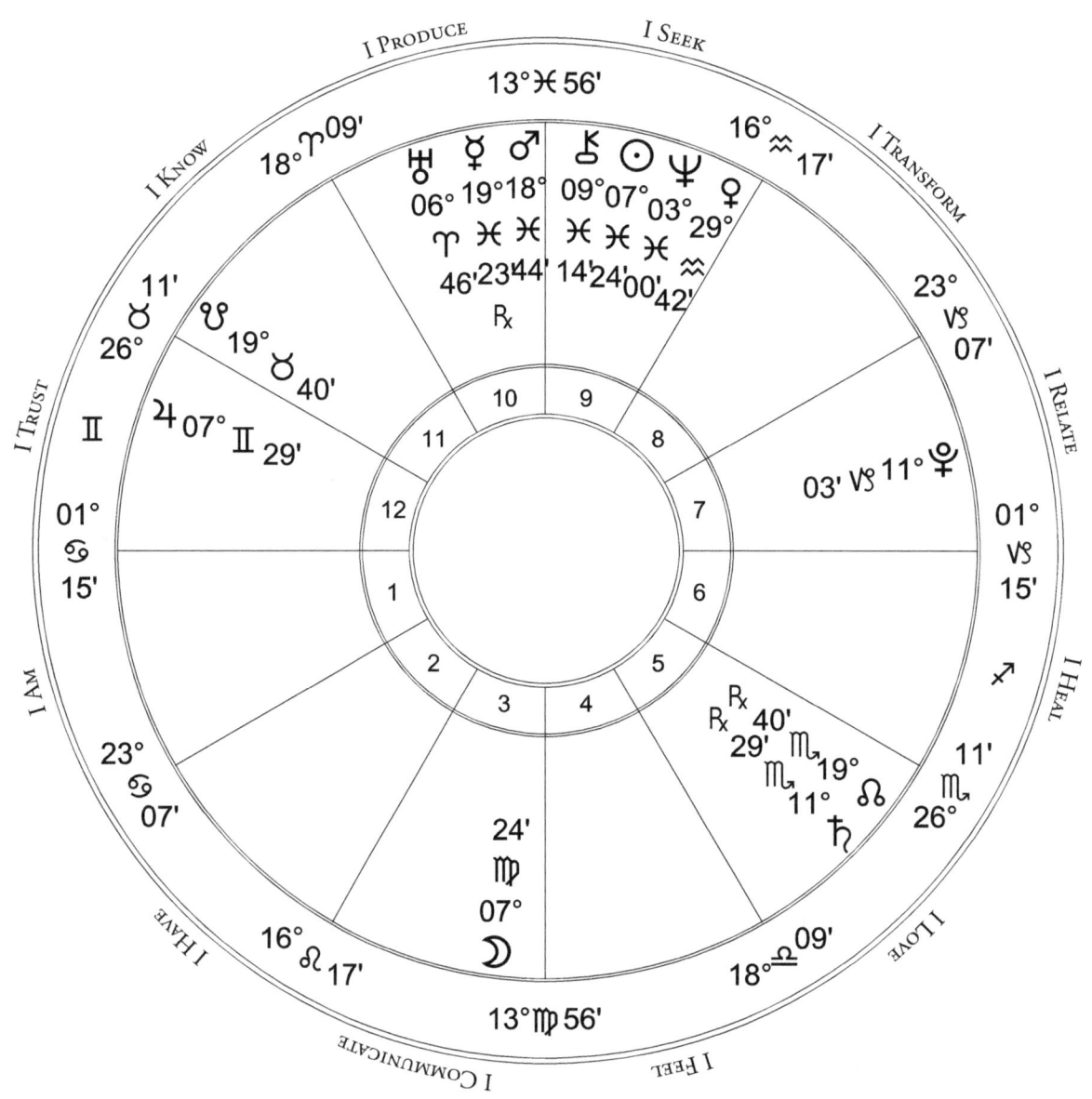

♈ Aries	♋ Cancer	♏ Scorpio	♓ Pisces	♀ Venus	♅ Uranus	☊ North Node
♉ Taurus	♌ Leo	♐ Sagittarius	☉ Sun	♂ Mars	♆ Neptune	☋ South Node
♊ Gemini	♍ Virgo	♑ Capricorn	☽ Moon	♃ Jupiter	♀ or ♇ Pluto	℞ Retrograde
	♎ Libra	♒ Aquarius	☿ Mercury	♄ Saturn	⚷ Chiron	

44

full Moon in Virgo

February 25, 12:26 PM

Cosmic Check-In

Take a moment to write a brief phrase for each "I" statement.
This activates all areas of your life for this freedom cycle.

♍ I Heal

♎ I Relate

♏ I Transform

♐ I Seek

♑ I Produce

♒ I Know

♓ I Trust

♈ I Am

♉ I Have

♊ I Communicate

♋ I Feel

♌ I Love

March 2013

SUN	MON	TUE	WED	THU	FRI	SAT
					1 ☿♄℞ ☽ → ♏ 9:34 AM 4. Make order your art form today.	**2** ☿♄℞ 5. Your health requires your ability to change.
3 ☿♄℞ ☽ V/C 1:20 AM ☽ → ♐ 1:12 PM 6. Love of others requires self-love.	**4** ☿♄℞▲ 7. Think with your heart and feel with your mind.	**5** ☿♄℞▲ ☽ V/C 7:29 AM ☽ → ♑ 4:15 PM 8. Celebrate someone else's success.	**6** ☿♄℞ 9. Enlightenment happens when you are ready.	**7** ☿♄℞ ☽ V/C 1:15 PM ☽ → ♒ 7:02 PM 10. See every day as a new beginning.	**8** ☿♄℞ ☽ V/C 2:09 PM 11. Be open to expressing more of who you are.	**9** ☿♄℞ ☽ → ♓ 12:19 PM 3. Happiness requires joyful living.
10 ☿♄℞ PDT BEGINS 4. Loyalty generates more trust.	**11** ☿♄℞ ● 21°♓24′ 12:54 PM ♂ → ♈ 11:27 PM ☽ V/C 12:52 PM 5. Exercise at least 15 minutes a day.	**12** ☿♄℞ ☽ → ♈ 4:18 AM 6. Freedom requires being fully present.	**13** ☿♄℞ ☽ V/C 1:03 AM 7. The mind can lie, the body doesn't.	**14** ☿♄℞ ☽ → ♉ 12:09 PM 8. Understanding creates love.	**15** ☿♄℞ 10. Let go of the past.	**16** ☿♄℞ ☽ V/C 4:12 PM ☽ → ♊ 11:10 PM 11. Be willing to let go and move on.
17 ♄℞ St. Patrick's Day ☿SD-5°♓38′ - 1:04 PM 3. Take time to play today.	**18** ♄℞▼ 4. Find your personal point of balance.	**19** ♄℞▼ ☽ V/C 10:28AM ☽ → ♋ 11:56 AM 5. Know that you make a difference.	**20** ♄℞ Spring Equinox ☉ → ♈ 4:03 AM ☽ V/C 11:03 AM 6. Generate harmony in all your relationships.	**21** ♄℞ ♀ → ♈ 8:16 PM ☽ → ♌ 11:51 PM 7. Immediately stop a negative thought.	**22** ♄℞ ☽ V/C 8:29 PM 8. Manifestation requires action.	**23** ♄℞ 9. Pray out loud, not in your mind.
24 ♄℞ Palm Sunday ☽ → ♍ 8:50 AM 10. See each day as a fresh new start.	**25** ♄℞ ☽ V/C 5:46 AM 11. The Universe gives you unlimited options.	**26** ♄℞ Passover ☽ → ♎ 2:33 PM 3. Find a way to play today.	**27** ♄℞ ○ 6°♎52′ 2:28 AM ☽ V/C 11:15 AM 4. Know the system that works for you.	**28** ♄℞ ☽ → ♏ 5:54 PM 5. Make a change that works for you.	**29** ♄℞ Good Friday ☽ V/C 1:26 PM 6. Freshen up a room in your home.	**30** ♄℞ ☽ → ♐ 8:14 PM 7. To understand, look more deeply.
31 ♄℞ Easter ☽ V/C 10:01 PM 8. Thank the Universe for your abundance.						

March 2013 Planetary Highlights

Saturn will be retrograde in Scorpio for the entire month

We will be looking at what we keep hidden from ourselves and others. Begin to notice where an impulsive action took you on a detour away from your boundaries. See what you can do to retrace the impulse and update it by asking how to take responsibility for the action. It is reconciliation time.

Mercury continues to be retrograde in Leo until the 17th of the month

Loving communication is up for review. See where you hold yourself back from truly and freely sharing your love.

March 11 – Neptune, Mercury retrograde, and Chiron are tripled in Pisces

The mind could be clouded. Keep your mouth shut unless you have a clear view about what you are saying and that the person you are talking to has a clear head as well. Wounds are deep and very present in people right now, so misinterpretation and being misunderstood could really hurt. A positive approach to this pattern would be to hold the space for a major discovery to occur in the healing.

March 11 – Mars in Pisces and Uranus in Aries are Dancing Together

This is a highly energetic transit. Expect a drive taking over to finish projects and get on to the next one. Adventure is in the air! You may feel a strong urge to go sky-diving, deep sea diving, mountain climbing, or fly a glider. The mind will soar way beyond the norm, enjoy! Watch out for rebellion to take over if you get stuck inside a box.

March 18, 11:27 PM – Mars enters Aries

At long last, Mars is comfortable at home. Expect action, change, variety, expansion, and travel ideas to come forward without blockage. Breakthrough is a reality now! Go! Go! Go!

March 20, 4:03 AM – Sun enters Aries (Spring Equinox)

This marks the time and space for new life to begin on the planet. Expect an infusion of light to inspire you to live freely and fully. Dreamtime is officially over—awakening is here now!

March 21st, 8:16 PM – Venus enters Aries

This is an extremely impulsive energy. If channeled in a focused manner, an abundance of creative projects can evolve at a very fast pace. If not, the impulsive action could get you in trouble, especially in the relationship area. This could leave you with some regrets to be dealt with later. Make love, not war!

March 27th Venus, Sun, Mars, and Uranus in Aries are joined opposing the Moon in Libra

Yikes! This adds a very energized and frenzied approach to relationship. Expect to have a deep desire to be free if you are already involved. If not, your attraction force will bring you to unusual and perhaps extreme action with very different kinds of people. Beware! This off-the-wall experience will be very exciting and short-lived, yet may have long range regrets.

March 27th Neptune, Mercury, and Chiron still in Pisces conjunct

The best use of this pattern is to communicate with the Divine about how to heal the hearts of all religions. Meditation is a perfect way to connect. There is a really good channel available right now for healing and mediumship. If used correctly, even miracles can happen! Start a group or join one to keep the channel clear.

March 4 and 5 – Super-Sensitivity ▲

Chaos is in the air. Make sure you 'go with the flow' at a pace that works for you. The speed of this transit could make accidents happen. Pace yourself. Avoid travel, if possible, especially by air. Expect rearrangement of plans. Stay grounded to avoid depression.

March 18 and 19 – Low-Vitality ▼

Expect endings to become apparent, resisting them will burn you out. Simply say goodbye to what is ending to insure the arrival of a new beginning. The body needs extra attention; get rest and drink lots of water. Earth changes are possible at this time.

♈ Aries	♋ Cancer	♐ Sagittarius	☽ Moon	♄ Saturn	☊ North Node	V/C Void-of-Course
♉ Taurus	♌ Leo	♑ Capricorn	☿ Mercury	♅ Uranus	☋ South Node	▲ Super-Sensitivity
♊ Gemini	♍ Virgo	♒ Aquarius	♀ Venus	♆ Neptune	➔ Enters	▼ Low-Vitality
	♎ Libra	♓ Pisces	♂ Mars	♀ or ♇ Pluto	℞ Retrograde	
	♏ Scorpio	☉ Sun	♃ Jupiter	⚷ Chiron	S/D Stationary Direct	

new Moon in Pisces

March 11, 12:54 PM

Statement I Trust
Body Feet
Mind Knowing your path
Spirit Universal consciousness

When the Sun is in Pisces

This is a time when we come in contact with our most Divine essence. It is a time to meditate and connect to your higher purpose. Let your intuition guide you to a program of service. Let your Soul take control and connect to a space beyond your ego. In order to do this, we must become free of our habits, hang ups, and fantasies. Compassion frees us from the slavery of self-interest and the lure of our personality's blind urges, emotional traps, and mental crystallizations. When the Soul takes control, we unite our personality with Divine essence and radiate the light needed to find our true pathway.

Pisces Co-Creation Ideas

Now is the time to focus on...

- Connection with the Divine
- Creativity
- Healing powers
- Psychic abilities
- Sensitivity
- Compassion
- Service

Pisces Goddess

Pisces Goddess Kuan Yin is the embodiment of all that is compassionate. She guides us to the abyss, a place known as emptiness. This place is called the Great Unknown, where the ego drops and there is only the truth of one's nature. Kuan Yin protects us, and holds us when we let go, surrender, and evolve. She is the goddess of emptiness. She helps to constantly empty the self from the limitations of the ego—fear, doubt, guilt, shame, and denial. In exchange, we gain beauty, light, and service. She is often pictured riding on the head of a dragon. It is the breath of the dragon that pierces the veil of illusion.

On Your Altar

Colors: Turquoise, blue, green, aqua

Numerology: 5 – Expand your exercise routine

Tarot Card: The Moon – the inner journey, reflection, illumination

Gemstones: Amethyst, opal, jade, turquoise

Plant Remedy: Passion flower – the ability to live in the here and now

Fragrance: Lotus – connecting to the Divine without arrogance

New Moon in Pisces

March 11, 12:54 PM

Pisces Challenges and Victories

I see my path clearly now. I know I must walk by myself on this journey into the deepest part of my Soul. It is time to clear the way and look beneath the surface to discover the parts of myself that I have placed in the unconscious world to be worked on at a later date. That later date is now. I am aware that the postponement of my inner reality can no longer be delayed.

Evolution is pulling me and it has become greater than my distractions, my fear, my denial, and my refusal to face what I have hidden from myself and others. I am aware of outside influences that pull me away from facing my inner realms. I know without a doubt that I am only as sick as the secrets I keep from myself and others. I see clearly how these distractions, illusions, and secrets need to be recognized so I can find the separated parts of myself that have been left in the dark, obscured from the light. I know that it is time to bring myself into wholeness and bring my shadow side to the light of my awareness.

I begin by closing my eyes and experiencing darkness. I imagine myself on a lonely road, in the dark, walking alone. I pay particular attention to the sensations in my body and allow for the body to guide me to the places of dullness, numbness, fear, and anxiety. I simply allow for the intelligence of the body to coordinate the feeling with an image, person, or an event. I stay still and know from the depth of my being that recognition is all that is required of me right now. When recognition occurs, the light of awareness is ignited and the conscious world will take care of the rest. I know that the road to enlightenment requires me to first take the road into the dark side of my Soul.

Pisces Homework

Pisces co-creates by using her psychic powers for counseling, therapy, hypnosis, the ministry, and creating spiritual schools or healing centers. She is also successful in visionary arts, acting, music, medical and pharmaceutical fields, and oceanography.

Take time to go within to discover where new pathways are open for advancement. Blessings pour forth to those who move toward these pathways in the spirit of service. Be open to these pathways and consider the ones that benefit our planet with new ideas, creative expression, and expanded views that lead people to higher levels of service.

New Moon in Pisces

March 11, 12:54 PM

Five Steps to Co-Creation

1. Acceptance

Acceptance opens the pathway to living in the moment and makes way for opportunity to occur. Co-creation can only occur when you live in the moment.

Start your list by writing... "I accept _____ into my life."

2. Adjustment

Consider what adjustments you may need to make in order to receive what you are accepting into your life.

My Co-Creation List

New Moon in Pisces

March 11, 12:54 PM

3. Awakening

Once your list is complete, use the power of sound and read your list out loud. This directs your intentions (your list) toward actualization and co-creation.

4. Alignment

Now it is time to make a petition to the Universe, using these words, "I call on the power of the Universe to know I am ready to receive my list. I accept it. I allow it. So be it! This, or something better than this, comes to me in an easy and pleasurable way for the good of all concerned. Thank You Universe!" Light your candle and place it on your eight-sided mirror.

5. Acknowledgement

When a creation result is acknowledged it seals the deal. This makes room for more magnificence to expand into your life and increases your abundance factor adding to your ability to receive.

As each aspect of your co-creation list arrives in your life, spend time allowing, acknowledging, and accepting it with the true gusto of gratitude. You might want to make a victory list here.

Victory List

Pisces Questions to ask Myself

How can I move through density and bloom to the fullness of my destiny?

What truth do I need to face about myself while staying connected to the Divine?

If I could claim mastery in my life, where would that be?

new Moon in Pisces

March 11, 12:54 PM

How to Use the Moon Book With Your Chart

Fill in the blanks on the Cosmic Check-In page. Then look up the degree of the moon on the chart below. Take note of the "I" statement on the outside of the wheel where the moon is located. Now locate the same degree on your own chart, and make a note of the house and corresponding "I" statement. Go back to the Cosmic Check-In page and circle the two statements from the charts and read what you wrote. This will give you an idea about what to expect from this moon phase on a personal level.

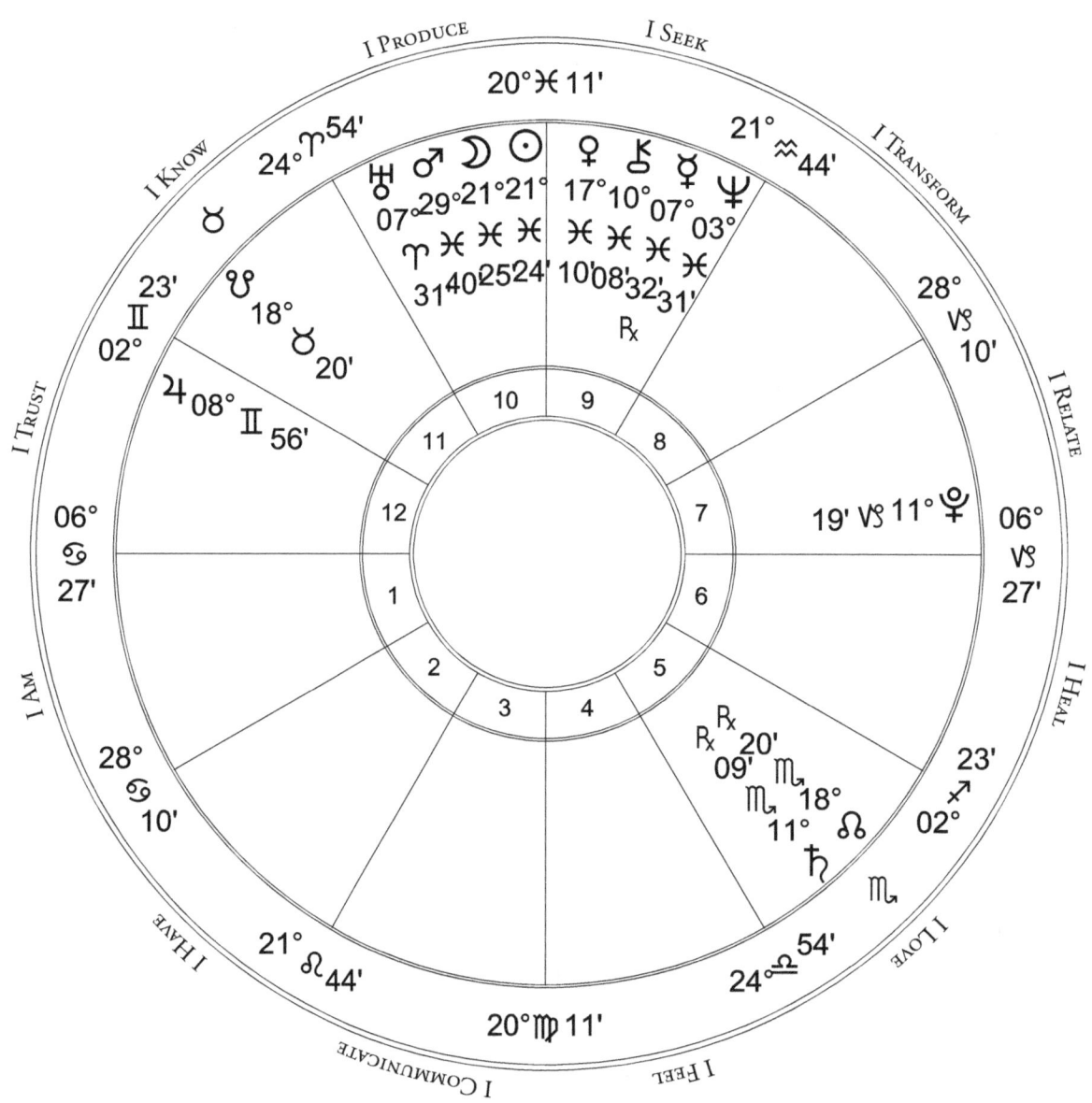

♈ Aries	♋ Cancer	♏ Scorpio	♓ Pisces	♀ Venus	♅ Uranus	☊ North Node
♉ Taurus	♌ Leo	♐ Sagittarius	☉ Sun	♂ Mars	♆ Neptune	☋ South Node
♊ Gemini	♍ Virgo	♑ Capricorn	☽ Moon	♃ Jupiter	♀ or ♇ Pluto	℞ Retrograde
	♎ Libra	♒ Aquarius	☿ Mercury	♄ Saturn	⚷ Chiron	

New Moon in Pisces

March 11, 12:54 PM

Cosmic Check-In

Take a moment to write a brief phrase for each "I" statement.
This activates all areas of your life for this creative cycle.

♓ I Trust

♈ I Am

♉ I Have

♊ I Communicate

♋ I Feel

♌ I Love

♍ I Heal

♎ I Relate

♏ I Transform

♐ I Seek

♑ I Produce

♒ I Know

Full Moon in Libra

March 27, 2:28 AM

Statement *I Relate*
Body *Kidneys*
Mind *Relationship*
Spirit *Peach*

The Sun is Opposite the Moon

Full Moons are always in opposition to the Sun. This creates a feeling of tension between where you want to shine and how your feelings are flowing on a sensory level about the Sun's directive. The two forces seem like they are working against each other, yet they are on the same team displaying different techniques to attain the same mission. The Libra/Aries polarity creates tension between the idea of "we" versus "me".

Libra Goddess

Athena was born out of her father's head. She was the first woman who incorporated logic into her consciousness. Her keen ability to combine logic and intuition gave birth to strategy. Because of her strategic concepts, she became a consort to all of the great warriors. Unlike Aries, who is the Warrior, Libra is the General. When the Moon is full in Libra, we must look at how strategy is working in our life. Has strategy become out of balance? Are we too removed from "our troops in the field?" It is time to balance our head with our heart.

Libra Freedom List Ideas

Now is the time to free myself from…

- Situations that are not balanced
- People-pleasing and the need to be liked
- Sorrow over past relationships
- Unsupportive relationships
- The need to be right
- False accusations
- Being misunderstood

On Your Altar

Colors: Pink, green

Numerology: 4 – Organization is the key to balance

Tarot Card: Justice – the ability to stay in the center of polarity

Gemstones: Rose quartz, jade

Plant Remedy: Olive trees – stamina

Fragrance: Eucalyptus – clarity of breath

Full Moon in Libra

March 27, 2:28 AM

Memory Maintenance Meditation

The Moon governs our memory and the maintenance of our memory. It is our memory that often creates blocks to setting us free to be able to attain our goals. The Moon works with us to help us become free from memory blocks three days after the Full Moon. The freedom themes are provided by the zodiac sign and can be from this lifetime or other lifetimes. These meditations assist in dissolving blocks and open pathways to new frontiers.

When the Moon is in Libra, the ego undergoes a research program looking for motives behind all action. Sit quietly and close your eyes. Breathe in and breathe out. Ask the Angel of Records to take you to a moment in time of perceived errors, miscarriage of justice, or false sense of self-guilt. Ask to be anointed by a cloister of Heavenly Saints so that false guilt can be removed and exchanged for forgiveness, and a full expression of feelings flowing in a friendly manner toward yourself and others.

Libra Challenges and Victories

I am awakened to the reality of the Law of Cause and Effect. I take time out today to see what is coming back to me. I know my actions, my words, and my thoughts have life and manifest in a pattern that returns to me. Today, I am in a place where I can clearly see the results of my words, my actions, and my thoughts. I am aware that it is time for a review and, in so doing, I am given the opportunity to balance, integrate and redistribute these results in a more productive way. When I truly know and experience the Law of Cause and Effect (what I put out comes back to me), I can truly take responsibility for my actions, words, and thoughts, and set myself free of blame. When blame is gone from my thought pattern (self-inflicted blame or circumstantial blame), I am able to benefit from my review rather than wasting energy justifying or defending my position. I now accept the idea that I am free to reconcile with whatever I have labeled as an injustice in my life. I take the time to re-route my thinking towards making life a beneficial experience. Today, I accept that in changing my language I can change my life. Today, I prepare to take actions toward beneficial experiences. Today, I release the need to be right and accept the right to be. Today, I stop judging life and start living life.

Libra Homework

Let the fresh air blow away mental stagnation related to times when you let others' interests supersede your own. Drink an excess amount of water to alert your kidneys that the freedom process has commenced. It's time to deepen your intention to be one with the light, promoting restoration on earth.

full Moon in Libra

March 27, 2:28 AM

Five Steps to Freedom

When we work with the concept of freedom we are soon presented with resistance. Freedom presents a pathway for us to bump directly into our limitations. When we can become aware of these limits, we can then find our way to freedom. Below are some ideas that might assist you in seeing deeper into your resistance to accepting freedom into your life. Once you discover these you might want to add more to your freedom list.

1. Feeling Useless

This happens when you measure yourself by what others think of you.

2. Discouragement

This occurs when you use blame others instead of taking responsibility for your part in a situation.

3. Regret

This happens when you live inside past events and continue to rehearse your story, hoping that if you tell it enough, it will get resolved. Living in the past leads to regret and blocks you from freedom.

4. Limitation

This happens when we think that there is no way out of a challenge, which creates an inability to see options. When options are out of the picture we become unable to create positive outcomes.

5. Self-Doubt

This takes place when we think that others are better than we are. Growing cannot occur when we have given someone else our ceiling.

full Moon in Libra

March 27, 2:28 AM

My Freedom List

Libra Questions to Ask Myself

Where am I most misunderstood?

Where do I let my need to be right keep me from living fully and freely?

Where do I stay in a relationship, just to be in one?

Full Moon in Libra

March 27, 2:28 AM

How to Use the Moon Book With Your Chart

Fill in the blanks on the Cosmic Check-In page. Then look up the degree of the moon on the chart below. Take note of the "I" statement on the outside of the wheel where the moon is located. Now locate the same degree on your own chart, and make a note of the house and corresponding "I" statement. Go back to the Cosmic Check-In page and circle the two statements from the charts and read what you wrote. This will give you an idea about what to expect from this moon phase on a personal level.

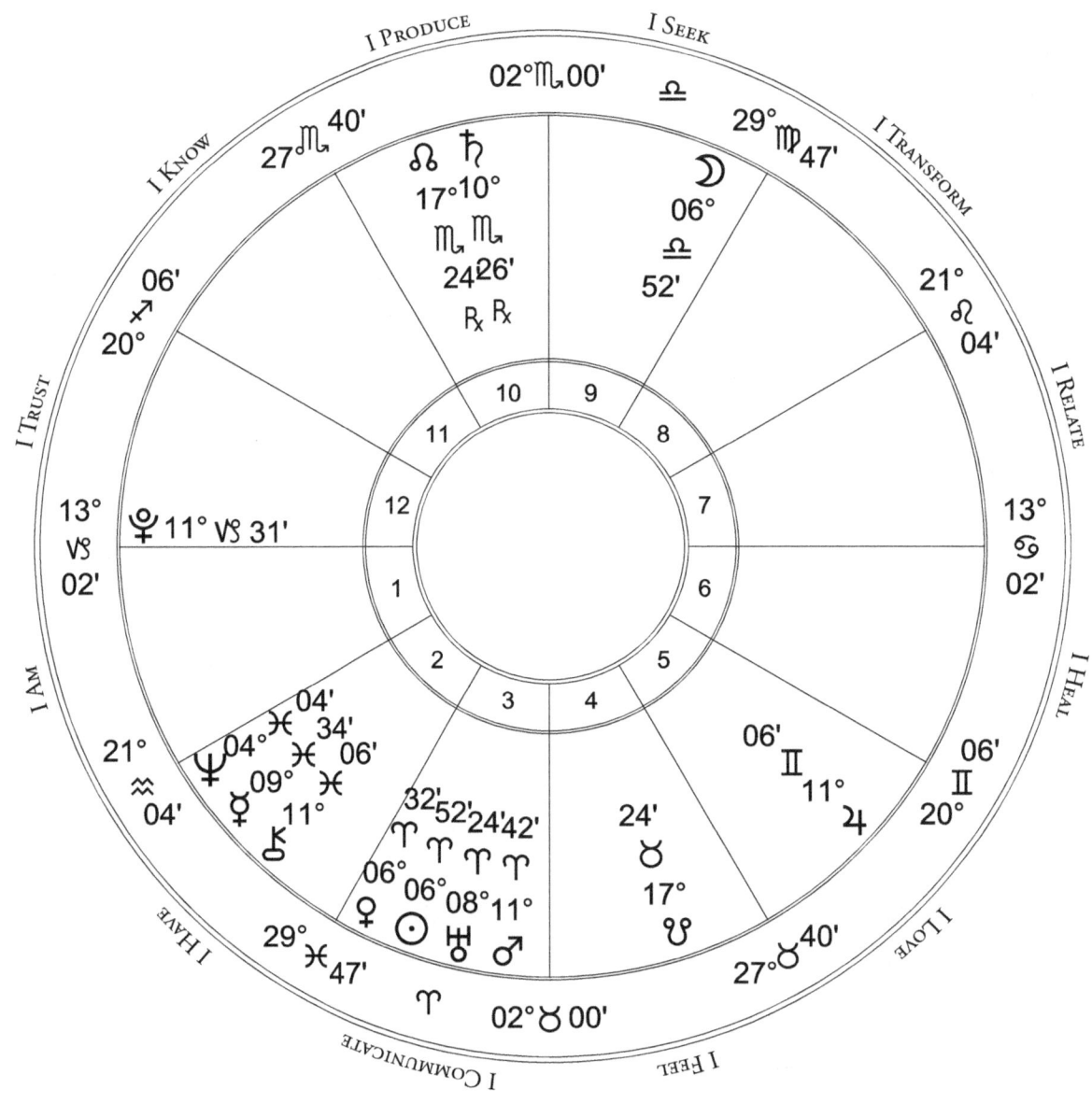

♈ Aries	♋ Cancer	♏ Scorpio	♓ Pisces	♀ Venus	♅ Uranus	☊ North Node
♉ Taurus	♌ Leo	♐ Sagittarius	☉ Sun	♂ Mars	♆ Neptune	☋ South Node
♊ Gemini	♍ Virgo	♑ Capricorn	☽ Moon	♃ Jupiter	♀ or ♇ Pluto	℞ Retrograde
	♎ Libra	♒ Aquarius	☿ Mercury	♄ Saturn	⚷ Chiron	

full Moon in Libra

March 27, 2:28 AM

Cosmic Check-In

Take a moment to write a brief phrase for each "I" statement.
This activates all areas of your life for this freedom cycle.

♎ I Relate

♏ I Transform

♐ I Seek

♑ I Produce

♒ I Know

♓ I Trust

♈ I Am

♉ I Have

♊ I Communicate

♋ I Feel

♌ I Love

♍ I Heal

April 2013

SUN	MON	TUE	WED	THU	FRI	SAT
	1 ♄℞▲ April Fools ☽ → ♑ 10:36 PM 9. Pray out loud for unity.	**2** ♄℞▲ 10. A bright new day awaits you.	**3** ♄℞ ☽ V/C 3:36 AM 11. There are no mistakes in the Universe.	**4** ♄℞ ☽ → ♒ 1:42 AM 3. Allow your truth to change as you do.	**5** ♄℞ ☽ V/C 10:23 AM 4. All systems are flexible.	**6** ♄℞ ☽ → ♓ 6:01 AM 5. To be healthy, be active.
7 ♄℞ ☽ V/C 9:11 PM 6. A healthy heart lives in harmony.	**8** ♄℞ ☽ → ♈ 12:03 PM 7. Quiet your mind and listen to your heart.	**9** ♄℞ 8. The more you share, the more you gain.	**10** ♄℞ 20°♈41' 2:36 AM ☽ V/C 9:26 AM ☽ → ♉ 8:23 PM 9. Honor the path each person walks.	**11** ♄℞ 10. Make your vision your reality.	**12** ♄♇℞ ♇℞—11°♑35' 12:33 PM 2. In all ways stay in balance.	**13** ♄♇℞ ☽ V/C 5:31 AM ☽ → ♊ 7:14 AM ☿ → ♈ 7:38 PM 3. Joy is your birth-right - live it!
14 ♄♇℞▼ 4. You are the best piece of the puzzle.	**15** ♄♇℞▼ ♀ → ♉ 12:26 AM ☽ V/C 12:42 PM ☽ → ♋ 7:50 PM 5. Make change your friend.	**16** ♄♇℞ 6. Choose flowers that reflect your personality.	**17** ♄♇℞ 7. Analyze some-thing in more depth.	**18** ♄♇℞ ☽ V/C 5:32 AM ☽ → ♌ 8:14 AM 8. Learn to receive as well as give.	**19** ♄♇℞ ☽ V/C 2:07 PM ☉ → ♉ 3:04 PM 9. Pay attention to your intuition.	**20** ♄♇℞ ♂ → ♉ 4:49 AM ☽ → ♍ 6:09 PM 10. Plan ahead and live in the moment.
21 ♄♇℞ ☽ V/C 11:03 PM 11. Remember you and the Universe are one.	**22** ♄♇℞ Earth Day 3. A playful attitude relaxes everyone.	**23** ♄♇℞ ☽ → ♎ 12:26 AM 4.The best approach is practical.	**24** ♄♇℞ ☽ V/C 5:13 AM 5. Daily exercise is a requirement.	**25** ♄♇℞ 5°♏46' 12:58 PM Lunar Eclipse 1:09 PM ☽ → ♏ 3:26 AM 6. Feel compas-sion in your heart.	**26** ♄♇℞ ☽ V/C 1:57 AM 7. You are smarter than you think.	**27** ♄♇℞ ☽ → ♐ 4:33 AM 8. Success is the result of action.
28 ♄♇℞ ☽ V/C 9:38 PM 9. Pray for highest and best good for others.	**29** ♄♇℞▲ ☽ → ♑ 5:22 AM 10. A bright future follows a happy now.	**30** ♄♇℞▲ 2. After you decide, take action.				

April 2013 Planetary Highlights

Saturn continues to be Retrograde in Scorpio all Month

Notice where resistance shows up to add to your need to control your outcomes. Much pain and many days of exhaustion could occur if you keep trying to break down walls by using brute force. When resistance arrives, transformation is very close. Simply know this and use this knowledge to trust that the Universe knows more than you do right now. Accept it, allow it ... so be it!

Saturn Retrograde and the North Node Retrograde are coupled in Scorpio

Pay attention to the manner in which you associate with others in terms of give-and-take. Expect irritable attitudes towards others. It's time to adopt a humbler approach to others. You might meet mentors or those older or wiser than you who have something important to teach you.

April 5, 12:26 AM – Venus enters Taurus

Sit in the lap of luxury and allow for abundance to be flowing your way. Shopping, spending, and collecting will take over and be on the top of your "To Do" list. Spend time in your garden feeling the plants flowering into their fullness.

April 10 – The Sun, Moon, Mars, and Venus Dancing Together in Aries

This is a major course in self-development. Take the directive from the Sun to get to know your light and where it is shining. This will motivate your pathway toward the new image you've been waiting to develop beyond what you have previously known about yourself. Look at the reflection, in the shadow of the light provided by the Moon, to become aware of how your past has kept you from shining. Use the dynamic power of Mars to move you to your new way of being and be willing to advance. Let Venus take you shopping so you can re-vamp your wardrobe to match the new you!

April 12 – Pluto goes Retrograde in Capricorn and Continues for the Entire Month

Expect a re-translation around your perception of wealth to happen. Allow yourself to feel the difference and hold the space by knowing that money may not be perceived in the same way. Remember abundance will always be there.

April 20, 4:49 AM – Mars enters Taurus

Mars is not comfortable with the slow pace of Taurus. In order to flow during this time, slow down, smell the roses, and all will be well. Best not to try to change anything right now or you might encounter stubbornness in yourself or others. Have the courage to trust this slowing down; it is Nature's way to remind you of beauty and time to refine the aesthetics in your life.

April 25 – Full Moon Lunar Eclipse Conjunct Saturn Retrograde in Scorpio

Saturn calls upon you to identify the weaker areas of your life, and to fix or strengthen them. Check-in to see what your emotional structure was in 1994. Remembering this will increase the power of the lunar eclipse for you.

April 25 – The Sun, Mars in Taurus opposing Moon, Saturn Retrograde in Scorpio

Take time to reflect on what you want back from life emotionally. You have left your needs out of the equation and it is time to update what you have been leaving out. This will put you in a more realistic state rather than a resentful one.

April 1 and 2 – Super-Sensitivity ▲

Watch out for chaotic influences in the atmosphere. You may feel the need to match the chaos and go too fast. This can lead to accidents of all kinds.

April 14 and 15 – Low-Vitality ▼

Earth changes are possible. Honor the Earth; have a ceremony. Send Gratitude for the awesome home she provides for us.

♈ Aries	♋ Cancer	♐ Sagittarius	☽ Moon	♄ Saturn	☊ North Node	V/C Void-of-Course
♉ Taurus	♌ Leo	♑ Capricorn	☿ Mercury	♅ Uranus	☋ South Node	▲ Super-Sensitivity
♊ Gemini	♍ Virgo	♒ Aquarius	♀ Venus	♆ Neptune	➔ Enters	▼ Low-Vitality
	♎ Libra	♓ Pisces	♂ Mars	♇ or ♇ Pluto	℞ Retrograde	
	♏ Scorpio	☉ Sun	♃ Jupiter	⚷ Chiron	S/D Stationary Direct	

New Moon in Aries

April 10, 2:36 AM

Statement I Am
Body Head and Face
Mind Ego
Spirit Awakening

When the Sun is in Aries

Aries awakens the dreamer from winter sleep and represents the raw energy of Spring, when the new shoots of life burst forth. Aries is the fundamental, straightforward approach to life. There is no challenge that is too great, no obstacle too daunting, and no rival too powerful for the Aries. Aries symbolizes initiation, leadership, strength, and potency. Competition and achievement are very important to Aries. Now is the time to be a pioneer and break all barriers to become the winner you are.

Aries Goddess

Aries goddess, Tara, is the goddess of sublime realization. She assists us in dispelling our fears in order to receive the gifts life has available to us. She was born from a star, sparking life into the dark waters of winter, becoming the first incarnation of water and fire. Thus, the birth of Spring emerges. Legend says that Buddha placed her in the deepest part of the forest to guarantee life and light to all. He claimed her as the Mother of all Buddhas, to be reborn countless lifetimes to guarantee enlightenment and compassion to all women. The Dalai Lama calls her the first "Women's Libber" because she is the symbol of the rebirth of the feminine and gives birth to enlightenment, as does Aries on the equinox.

Aries Co-Creation Ideas

Now is the time to focus on...

- Personality power
- Leadership
- Strength
- Self-acceptance
- Winning
- Courage
- Personal appearance
- Advancing to new frontiers

On Your Altar

Colors: Red, black, white

Numerology: 9 – pray for the highest and best good for all of life

Tarot Card: Emperor – success on all levels

Gemstones: Diamond, red jasper, coral, obsidian

Plant Remedy: Pomegranates, oak – planting new life and rooting new life

Fragrance: Ginger – the ability to ingest and digest life

New Moon in Aries

April 10, 2:36 AM

Aries Challenges and Victories

I am the author of my life. I accept that I am a winner and, in so doing, all doors are open to me. I hold the world in the palm of my hand and I know that there is not a mountain that I cannot climb. My ability to respond to life is in operation today and I direct my intention to bring me to the next level of achievement that I have determined for myself. The world and its systems are available for me to use as tools for my success and I use them with true excellence. I am organized and all systems are in place for me to make my mark on the world. I accept my structured ground state and my dynamic energy is ready to make headway through pure determination, action, planning, and power. I will manage this plan and know that the sequence of events provided support me to make a breakthrough today.

I am willing to make my plan and take action on it. I gather my support team together today to focus on the appropriate action and encourage each person in their area of excellence and production. I am a great leader and my dynamic power is a good resource for others to determine their own success formula. I am aware that all parts of my team are important and place value on all areas of performance required to manifest in the world. I know how to place people in their best areas of expertise so they can experience their own unique talent manifesting. Today, I honor my father for what he taught me by what he did or didn't do to encourage my ability to perform. I am the producer. I am the protector. I am the provider. I am the promoter. I am power. I am the author of my life.

Aries Homework

Aries co-creates best as a professional athlete, personal trainer or coach, martial arts expert, military professional, demolitions expert, fireworks manufacturer, wardrobe consultant, and through sales and promotions.

Merge your light and dark forces so balance can occur. Then, give shape to your feelings through creative forms and learn to live in the duality of your soul and watch your spirit soar! The embodiment of this duality connects us to the unity, a requirement for these times.

New Moon in Aries

April 10, 2:36 AM

Five Steps to Co-Creation

1. Acceptance

Acceptance opens the pathway to living in the moment and makes way for opportunity to occur. Co-creation can only occur when you live in the moment.

Start your list by writing… "I accept _____ into my life."

2. Adjustment

Consider what adjustments you may need to make in order to receive what you are accepting into your life.

My Co-Creation List

new Moon in Aries

April 10, 2:36 AM

3. Awakening

Once your list is complete, use the power of sound and read your list out loud. This directs your intentions (your list) toward actualization and co-creation.

4. Alignment

Now it is time to make a petition to the Universe, using these words, "I call on the power of the Universe to know I am ready to receive my list. I accept it. I allow it. So be it! This, or something better than this, comes to me in an easy and pleasurable way for the good of all concerned. Thank You Universe!" Light your candle and place it on your eight-sided mirror.

5. Acknowledgement

When a creation result is acknowledged it seals the deal. This makes room for more magnificence to expand into your life and increases your abundance factor adding to your ability to receive.

As each aspect of your co-creation list arrives in your life, spend time allowing, acknowledging, and accepting it with the true gusto of gratitude. You might want to make a victory list here.

Victory List

Aries Questions to ask Myself

Where do I get trapped in an illusion that keeps me from knowing my essential self?

Where do I still chase truths from outer sources and end up disappointed?

How can I drop my ego and still feel like myself?

new Moon in Aries

April 10, 2:36 AM

How to Use the Moon Book With Your Chart

Fill in the blanks on the Cosmic Check-In page. Then look up the degree of the moon on the chart below. Take note of the "I" statement on the outside of the wheel where the moon is located. Now locate the same degree on your own chart, and make a note of the house and corresponding "I" statement. Go back to the Cosmic Check-In page and circle the two statements from the charts and read what you wrote. This will give you an idea about what to expect from this moon phase on a personal level.

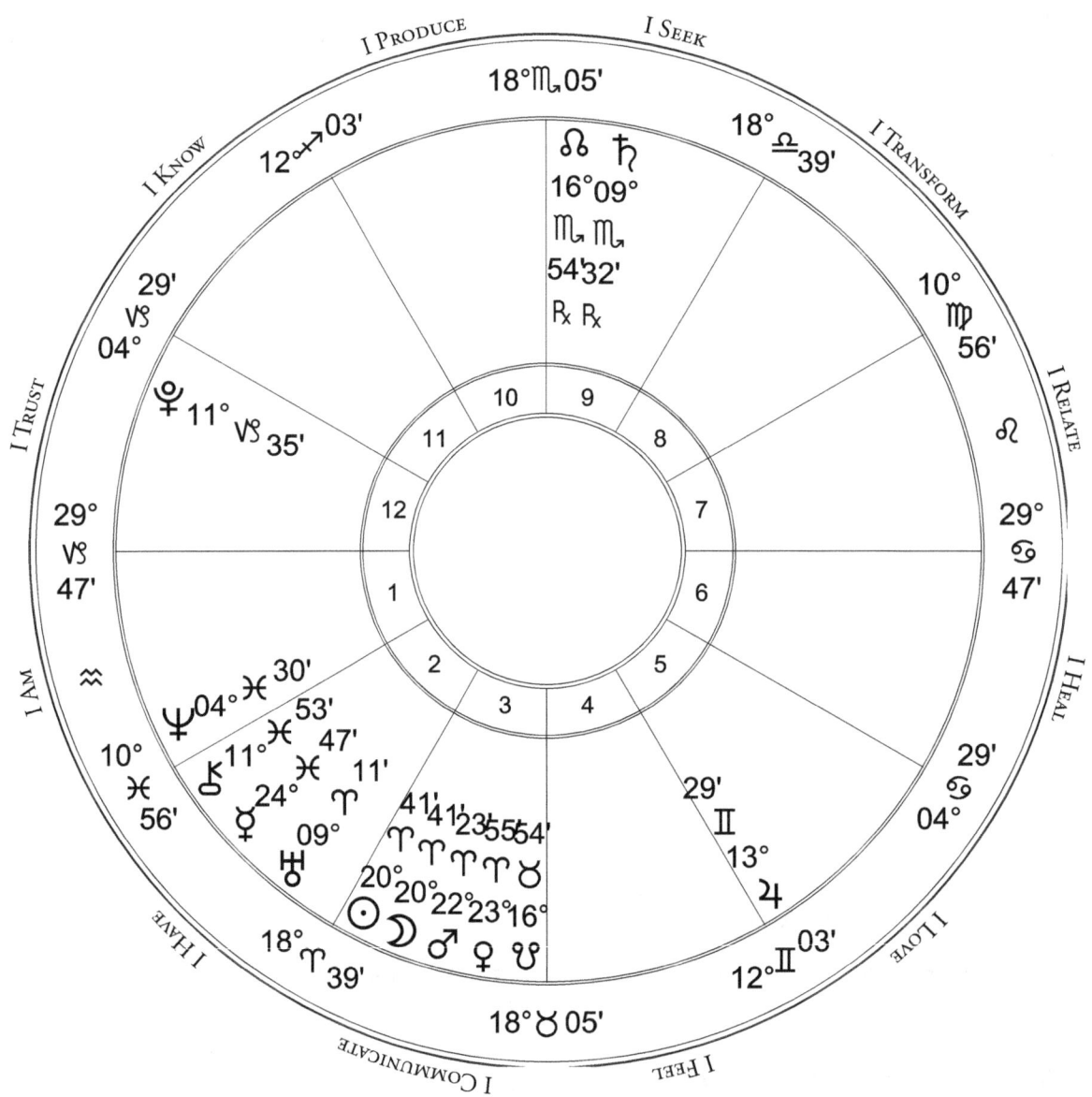

♈ Aries	♋ Cancer	♏ Scorpio	♓ Pisces	♀ Venus	♅ Uranus	☊ North Node
♉ Taurus	♌ Leo	♐ Sagittarius	☉ Sun	♂ Mars	♆ Neptune	☋ South Node
♊ Gemini	♍ Virgo	♑ Capricorn	☽ Moon	♃ Jupiter	♀ or ♇ Pluto	℞ Retrograde
♎ Libra		♒ Aquarius	☿ Mercury	♄ Saturn	⚷ Chiron	

new Moon in Aries

April 10, 2:36 AM

Cosmic Check-In

Take a moment to write a brief phrase for each "I" statement.
This activates all areas of your life for this creative cycle.

♈ I Am

♉ I Have

♊ I Communicate

♋ I Feel

♌ I Love

♍ I Heal

♎ I Relate

♏ I Transform

♐ I Seek

♑ I Produce

♒ I Know

♓ I Trust

Full Moon in Scorpio

April 25, 12:58 PM – Lunar Eclipse

Statement I Transform
Body Sex Organs
Mind Intensity
Spirit Transformation

The Sun is Opposite the Moon

Full Moons are always in opposition to the Sun. This creates a feeling of tension between where you want to shine and how your feelings are flowing on a sensory level about the Sun's directive. The two forces seem like they are working against each other, yet they are on the same team displaying different techniques to attain the same mission. The Scorpio/Taurus polarity creates tension between feeling deeply about shared resources and living abundantly for yourself.

Scorpio God

Pluto was one of the three remaining sons of Saturn who were not consumed by his wrath. The three brothers looked at the elements that Time could not consume: Air, Water, and Death. The three brothers chose their non-consumable domains. Jupiter took the air, Neptune the water and Pluto the grave or the underworld. Pluto means wealth in the Greek language and is defined as "invisible fullness." Pluto is the God of Wealth. Hidden assets belong to the underworld and cannot be consumed until they are brought above the ground. When the Moon is full in Scorpio, we are given the opportunity to shine the light on our own underworld and see what we are hiding on an unconscious level. Subjects that Pluto tends to keep hidden are death, taxes, money, legacies, and sex. Look deep within yourself to see what resentments, fears, or hidden agendas you might be harboring in these areas. Bring them forward above the ground, and into the light of day.

Scorpio Freedom List Ideas

Now is the time to free myself from…

- Resentment, jealousy, and revenge
- Joint financial situations
- Vendettas
- Betrayals
- Blocks to transformation
- Destructive relationships
- Resistance to changing paradigms
- Obstacles to having a healthy sex life
- Karma relating to all issues of power

On Your Altar

Colors: Indigo, deep purple, scarlet

Numerology: 6 – love and sensuality are high priority

Tarot Card: Death – the ability to make changes

Gemstones: Topaz, tanzanite, onyx, obsidian

Plant Remedy: Manzanita – prepares the body for transformation

Fragrance: Sandalwood – awakens your sensuality

Full Moon in Scorpio

April 25, 12:58 PM – Lunar Eclipse

Memory Maintenance Meditation

The Moon governs our memory and the maintenance of our memory. It is our memory that often creates blocks to setting us free to be able to attain our goals. The Moon works with us to help us become free from memory blocks three days after the Full Moon. The freedom themes are provided by the zodiac sign and can be from this lifetime or other lifetimes. These meditations assist in dissolving blocks and open pathways to new frontiers.

When the Moon is in Scorpio, it is time to contact an Angel of Transformation to move you beyond the unruly representatives of your lower nature, such as retaliation, revenge, dominance, and misappropriated sexual focus. Sit down quietly. Breathe in and breathe out. Ask for clarification of purpose and dedication without deviation. Work with the Angel of Transformation to assist you in freeing yourself from any judgment attached to indiscretions, and replace your field of awareness with appropriate focus, determination, and drive.

Scorpio Challenges and Victories

I will not compromise myself today. I know that transformation occurs when I stand tall in my truth, even if everything around me needs to die. I see death as a new beginning and know that in death comes new aliveness. I am willing to embrace transformation and open to the idea that change is in my favor. I know that in letting go, I give new life to myself. I am willing to accept that life is ever-changing and in a constant state of renewal; one cannot occur without the other.

Releasing is easy when I offer myself something new. When I allow for the motion of change to stay alive, I let go with one hand and receive with the other hand. The ever-present flow and motion keeps me alive and connected to the revitalizing power of Nature. When the power of Nature becomes apparent to me, I become aware that Nature abhors a vacuum. Rejuvenation is mine when I embrace change.

Scorpio Homework

The Scorpio Moon creates the urge within us to make life happen. Pay attention to these urges so you can prepare yourself toward greater action, intention, and purpose.

full Moon in Scorpio

April 25, 12:58 PM – Lunar Eclipse

Five Steps to Freedom

When we work with the concept of freedom we are soon presented with resistance. Freedom presents a pathway for us to bump directly into our limitations. When we can become aware of these limits, we can then find our way to freedom. Below are some ideas that might assist you in seeing deeper into your resistance to accepting freedom into your life. Once you discover these you might want to add more to your freedom list.

1. Feeling Useless

This happens when you measure yourself by what others think of you.

2. Discouragement

This occurs when you use blame others instead of taking responsibility for your part in a situation.

3. Regret

This happens when you live inside past events and continue to rehearse your story, hoping that if you tell it enough, it will get resolved. Living in the past leads to regret and blocks you from freedom.

4. Limitation

This happens when we think that there is no way out of a challenge, which creates an inability to see options. When options are out of the picture we become unable to create positive outcomes.

5. Self-Doubt

This takes place when we think that others are better than we are. Growing cannot occur when we have given someone else our ceiling.

Full Moon in Scorpio
April 25, 12:58 PM – Lunar Eclipse

My Freedom List

Scorpio Questions to Ask Myself

Where do I let my focus deviate and drive myself off course?

What keeps me from the deep intimate passionate connection I truly desire?

Where does my need to control make it difficult for me to share with others?

full Moon in Scorpio

April 25, 12:58 PM – Lunar Eclipse

How to Use the Moon Book With Your Chart

Fill in the blanks on the Cosmic Check-In page. Then look up the degree of the moon on the chart below. Take note of the "I" statement on the outside of the wheel where the moon is located. Now locate the same degree on your own chart, and make a note of the house and corresponding "I" statement. Go back to the Cosmic Check-In page and circle the two statements from the charts and read what you wrote. This will give you an idea about what to expect from this moon phase on a personal level.

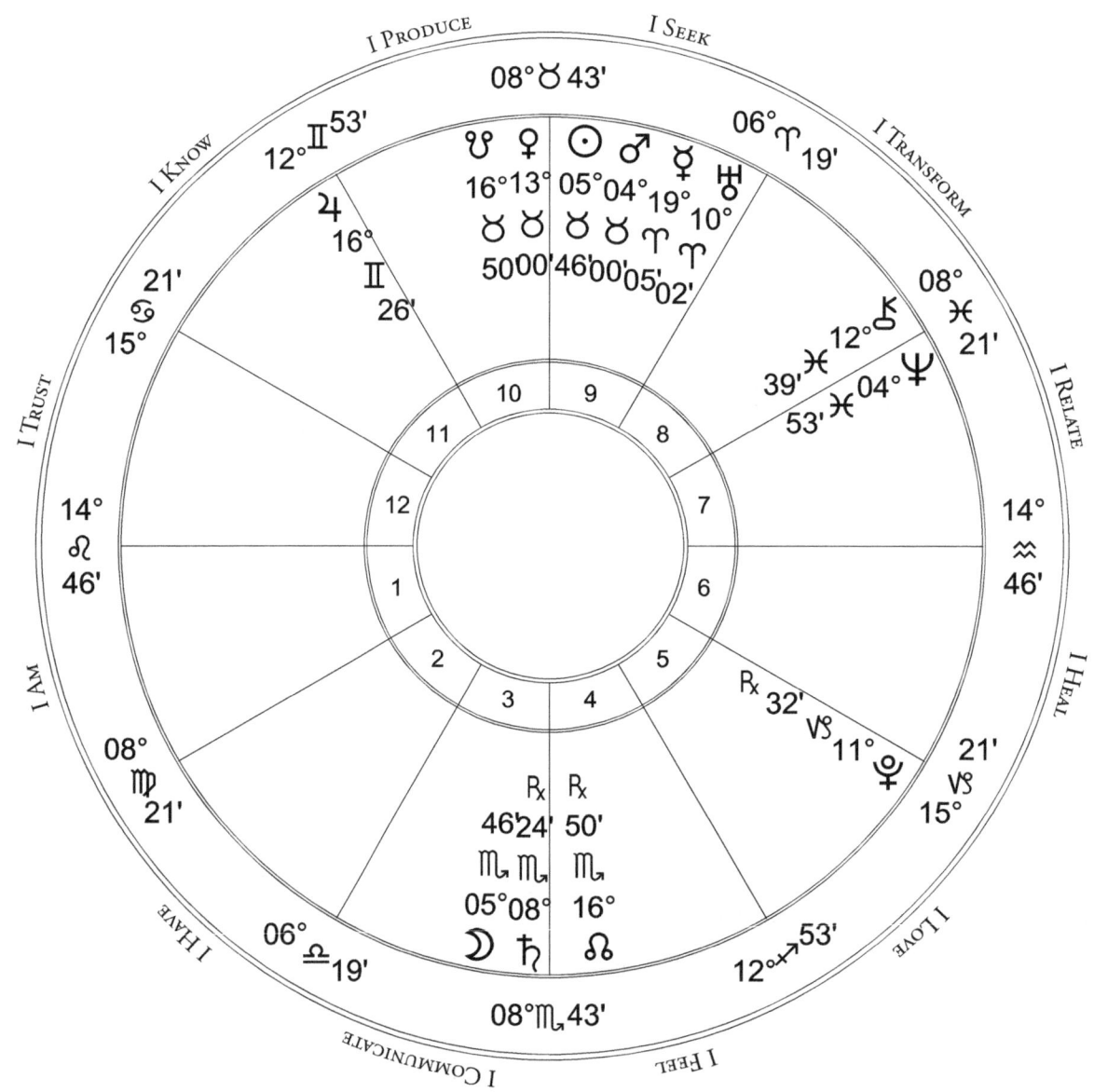

♈ Aries	♋ Cancer	♏ Scorpio	♓ Pisces	♀ Venus	⛢ Uranus	☊ North Node
♉ Taurus	♌ Leo	♐ Sagittarius	☉ Sun	♂ Mars	♆ Neptune	☋ South Node
♊ Gemini	♍ Virgo	♑ Capricorn	☽ Moon	♃ Jupiter	♀ or ♇ Pluto	℞ Retrograde
	♎ Libra	♒ Aquarius	☿ Mercury	♄ Saturn	⚷ Chiron	

full Moon in Scorpio

April 25, 12:58 PM – Lunar Eclipse

Cosmic Check-In

Take a moment to write a brief phrase for each "I" statement.
This activates all areas of your life for this freedom cycle.

♏ I Transform

♐ I Seek

♑ I Produce

♒ I Know

♓ I Trust

♈ I Am

♉ I Have

♊ I Communicate

♋ I Feel

♌ I Love

♍ I Heal

♎ I Relate

May 2013

SUN	MON	TUE	WED	THU	FRI	SAT
			1 ♄℞ ♀℞ May Day ☽ V/C 7:08 AM ☽ → ♒ 7:21 AM ♀ → ♉ 8:38 AM 3. Formulate your own belief system.	**2** ♄℞ ♀℞ ☽ V/C 9:25 PM 4. Be dependable, not dependent.	**3** ♄℞ ♀℞ ☽ → ♓ 11:26 AM 5. A change of pace is a good idea.	**4** ♄℞ ♀℞ 6. Candles enhance a romantic mood.
5 ♄℞ ♀℞ Cinco de Mayo ☽ V/C 9:01 AM ☽ → ♈ 6:04 PM 7. Trust your intuitive thoughts.	**6** ♄℞ ♀℞ 8. Be the leader you are looking for.	**7** ♄℞ ♀℞ ☽ V/C 5:41 AM 9. Prayers are very good medicine.	**8** ♄℞ ♀℞ ☽ → ♉ 3:10 AM 10. Create the energy for your future.	**9** ♄℞ ♀℞ ● 19°♉31' 5:29 PM ☽ V/C 5:29 PM Solar Eclipse 5:26 PM ♀ → ♊ 8:04 AM 2. Don't think - use thought.	**10** ♄℞ ♀℞ ☽ → ♊ 2:22 PM 3. A playful disposition makes life happier.	**11** ♄℞ ♀℞ 4. Release unworkable systems.
12 ♄℞ ♀℞ ▼ Mother's Day ☽ V/C 6:33 AM 5. Give flexibility a chance.	**13** ♄℞ ♀℞ ▼ ☽ → ♋ 2:58 AM 6. Create harmony by adapting.	**14** ♄℞ ♀℞ 7. Do something mentally stimulating.	**15** ♄℞ ♀℞ ☽ V/C 5:15 AM ☿ → ♊ 1:42 PM ☽ → ♌ 3:39 PM 8. There is more than enough to go around.	**16** ♄℞ ♀℞ 9. Find emotional strength through prayer.	**17** ♄℞ ♀℞ ☽ V/C 9:36 PM 10. Every death is a new beginning.	**18** ♄℞ ♀℞ ☽ → ♍ 2:34 AM 2. Action follows thought.
19 ♄℞ ♀℞ 3. Experience is your best teacher.	**20** ♄℞ ♀℞ ☽ V/C 9:49 AM ☽ → ♎ 10:08 AM ☉ → ♊ 2:11 PM 4. Find time for both work and play.	**21** ♄℞ ♀℞ 5. Travel a different path today.	**22** ♄℞ ♀℞ ☽ V/C 12:36 AM ☽ → ♏ 1:56 PM 6. Visit someone who is lonely.	**23** ♄℞ ♀℞ 7. Expand beyond limited thinking.	**24** ♄℞ ♀℞ ○ 4°♐08' 9:26 PM Lunar Eclipse 9:11 PM ☽ V/C 6:56 AM ☽ → ♐ 2:50 PM 8. Be open to working in new and rewarding ways.	**25** ♄℞ ♀℞ ▲ 9. Sing with joy in your heart.
26 ♄℞ ♀℞ ▲ ☽ V/C 3:23 AM ☽ → ♑ 2:29 PM 10. Planning is half the fun of a vacation.	**27** ♄℞ ♀℞ Memorial Day 3. Set aside a whole day for play.	**28** ♄℞ ♀℞ ☽ V/C 11:41 AM ☽ → ♒ 2:49 PM 4. Replace competition with cooperation.	**29** ♄℞ ♀℞ 5. Exercise on a regular basis.	**30** ♄℞ ♀℞ ☽ V/C 4:58 PM ☽ → ♓ 5:31 PM 6. Count your friends among your blessings.	**31** ♄℞ ♀℞ ☿ → ♋ 12:08 AM ♂ → ♊ 3:40 AM 7. Read something mentally stimulating.	

May 2013 Planetary Highlights

Saturn Retrograde in Scorpio all Month

You're likely to find that financial support is easier to come by as long as you are carefully watching your spending and borrowing habits. Honesty and responsibility are paramount especially where shared resources are concerned.

Pluto Retrograde in Capricorn all Month

Work on reformatting your daily routine to see where changes need to be made in your life. As you re-work your idea of time, let yourself feel how different it is and then see if you can establish a new tempo for being useful. Transform your point of view to become more flexible by widening your horizon to include something new for your business accomplishments.

May 1, 8:38 AM – Mercury enters Taurus

Mercury has to slow down the mind when it moves into Taurus. This is a time when the senses need to be expressed and integrated. Celebrating beauty is in the foreground and an awakening requires acceptance rather than a quick judgment. It's time to become one with all of life.

May 9, 8:04 AM – Venus enters Gemini

Expect conversations to be enchanting. It is time to flirt and be clever. Party time!

May 9 – The Sun, Moon, Mercury, South Node, and Mars are all Dancing in Taurus

Acquisition is hitting on many levels and from all directions right now. Be ready to receive and accept the abundance that is in the air and ready to land on Earth. Allow yourself to awaken to what is in front of you, within you, and behind you that is fruitful and ready to be yours. Be One with all of life.

May 9 – The Sun, Moon, Mercury, South Node, Mars conjunct in Taurus opposing North Node

This could create a tug of war between your past and your future, your inner-self and your outer-self, and your mind and your body. All areas for manifesting are open and require a multi-dimensional awakening in order to receive.

May 15, 1:42 PM – Mercury enters Gemini

The mind will move into high speed. Your ability to think will have a clarity that will come in very handy for making a sales pitch, doing research, presenting an idea, and inventing a gadget or two.

May 20, 2:11 PM – The Sun enters Gemini

Your message is important at this time. Make You Tube videos, send out proposals, create a newsletter, and write that book that you have been putting off. The power of the word is your tool for abundance, use it.

May 25 – Jupiter, Mercury, and Venus are all Hanging out in Gemini

Allow the mind to stay in a neutral place, beyond judgment, so that the power of the word and the Law Of Sound can direct abundance, benefits, and luxury your way … more miracles are on their way!

May 31, 12:08 AM – Mercury enters Cancer

This is where emotions meet thoughts, if used wisely you can give expression to your feelings like you never have before and let your truth set you free.

May 31, 3:40 AM – Mars enters Gemini

Expect high energy to move you to a new level on the board game of life! Take on a new sport, a new dance class, or join a new gym. Action, travel and expansion are top priority.

May 26 and 27 – Super-Sensitivity ▲

Watch out for negative thinking that is in the atmosphere right now. Remember, it is global, not personal. Hold the space for the highest and best good for the Cosmos.

May 12 and 13 – Low-Vitality ▼

Overdrive is in the equation right now. Slow down and use timing and tempo to guide your activities. Take a nap when needed.

♈ Aries	♋ Cancer	♐ Sagittarius	☽ Moon	♄ Saturn	☊ North Node	V/C Void-of-Course
♉ Taurus	♌ Leo	♑ Capricorn	☿ Mercury	⛢ Uranus	☋ South Node	▲ Super-Sensitivity
♊ Gemini	♍ Virgo	♒ Aquarius	♀ Venus	♆ Neptune	→ Enters	▼ Low-Vitality
	♎ Libra	♓ Pisces	♂ Mars	♀ or ♇ Pluto	℞ Retrograde	
	♏ Scorpio	☉ Sun	♃ Jupiter	⚷ Chiron	S/D Stationary Direct	

New Moon in Taurus

May 9, 5:29 PM – Solar Eclipse

Statement I Have
Body Neck
Mind Concrete Refinement
Spirit Bridge Heaven and Earth

When the Sun is in Taurus

Taurus is the time when we see the true manifesting power, as the plants move to a higher aspiration of life and bloom. Once again, we become connected to the essence of beauty as a symbol of our divinity. Taurus is the connection between humanity and divinity. Taurus' job is to infuse matter with light through accumulating layers of substance. This is why they are such good shoppers and collectors. The more they accumulate; the more divinity they experience. This process brings about a sense of self-value which is directly commensurate to the amount of money they manifest. Personal resources are part of the pattern. Discover your value at this time.

Taurus Co-Creation Ideas

Now is the time to focus on...

- Success
- Money
- Property
- Luxury
- Beauty
- Personal Value
- Pleasure
- Manifestation

Taurus Goddess

Taurus goddess, Lakshmi, is the goddess of wealth, abundance, and luxury. Lakshmi is the embodiment of power, fortune, and beauty. She was born out of an ocean of milk. When churned, the alchemy of manifestation turned the milk to butter and a symbol of wealth came into being. She sits on the lotus to remind us to be aware of the stages of evolution required for manifestation, infusing matter with light. Her hands are filled with symbols that show the four stages of manifestation: purpose, wealth, bodily pleasures, and beatitude. The more attention you give Lakshmi in the form of prayer, the wealthier you become.

On Your Altar

Colors: Green, pink, deep red, earth tones
Numerology: 2 – don't think, use thought
Tarot Card: Hierophant – the ability to listen, inner-knowing
Gemstones: Topaz, agate, smoky quartz, jade, rose quartz
Plant Remedy: Angelica – connecting Heaven and Earth
Fragrance: Rose – opening the heart

new Moon in Taurus

May 9, 5:29 PM – Solar Eclipse

Taurus Challenges and Victories

Everything is possible for me today. My possibilities are endless. I have the power within me to make all of my dreams come true. I have the tools to make my talent a reality. I have the power to identify with my talent. Today, I focus my attention and intention on manifesting with my talent and, in so doing, I transform my ideas into reality. I recognize the part of me that is connected to the cosmic source of ideas and I express that source within me to manifest my creative power. I see my possibilities and act on them today. I am the creative power. I am all-knowing. I am an individual. There is no one else like me. I can manifest anything I desire. I intend it, I allow it, so be it.

Rules for Manifesting

Know what you want. Write it down. Say it out loud. Recognize that because you thought it, it can be so. Release your limiting beliefs. Override your limiting beliefs with power statements. Act as if you have already manifested your idea. Lastly, value yourself!

Taurus Homework

Taurus co-creates best when buying, selling, and owning real estate, gardening and landscaping, selling and collecting art, manufacturing and selling fine furniture, singing or acting, and as a restaurateur, antique dealer, or interior designer.

The Moon in Taurus asks us to infuse light into form and, in so doing, the bridge between humanity and divinity is manifested and we can assume our stewardship in the physical world. When we release Spirit into matter, we become open to the idea that accumulation and actualization set us free to experience the abundance available to us here on Earth. Go shopping!

New Moon in Taurus

May 9, 5:29 PM – Solar Eclipse

Five Steps to Co-Creation

1. Acceptance

Acceptance opens the pathway to living in the moment and makes way for opportunity to occur. Co-creation can only occur when you live in the moment.

Start your list by writing… "I accept _____ into my life."

2. Adjustment

Consider what adjustments you may need to make in order to receive what you are accepting into your life.

My Co-Creation List

new Moon in Taurus

May 9, 5:29 PM – Solar Eclipse

3. Awakening

Once your list is complete, use the power of sound and read your list out loud. This directs your intentions (your list) toward actualization and co-creation.

4. Alignment

Now it is time to make a petition to the Universe, using these words, "I call on the power of the Universe to know I am ready to receive my list. I accept it. I allow it. So be it! This, or something better than this, comes to me in an easy and pleasurable way for the good of all concerned. Thank You Universe!" Light your candle and place it on your eight-sided mirror.

5. Acknowledgement

When a creation result is acknowledged it seals the deal. This makes room for more magnificence to expand into your life and increases your abundance factor adding to your ability to receive.

As each aspect of your co-creation list arrives in your life, spend time allowing, acknowledging, and accepting it with the true gusto of gratitude. You might want to make a victory list here.

Victory List

Taurus Questions to ask Myself

How can I be a good steward for the Earth's passage to a greater expression?

How does being valuable apply to me?

How is my body expressing its divinity?

new Moon in Taurus

May 9, 5:29 PM – Solar Eclipse

How to Use the Moon Book With Your Chart

Fill in the blanks on the Cosmic Check-In page. Then look up the degree of the moon on the chart below. Take note of the "I" statement on the outside of the wheel where the moon is located. Now locate the same degree on your own chart, and make a note of the house and corresponding "I" statement. Go back to the Cosmic Check-In page and circle the two statements from the charts and read what you wrote. This will give you an idea about what to expect from this moon phase on a personal level.

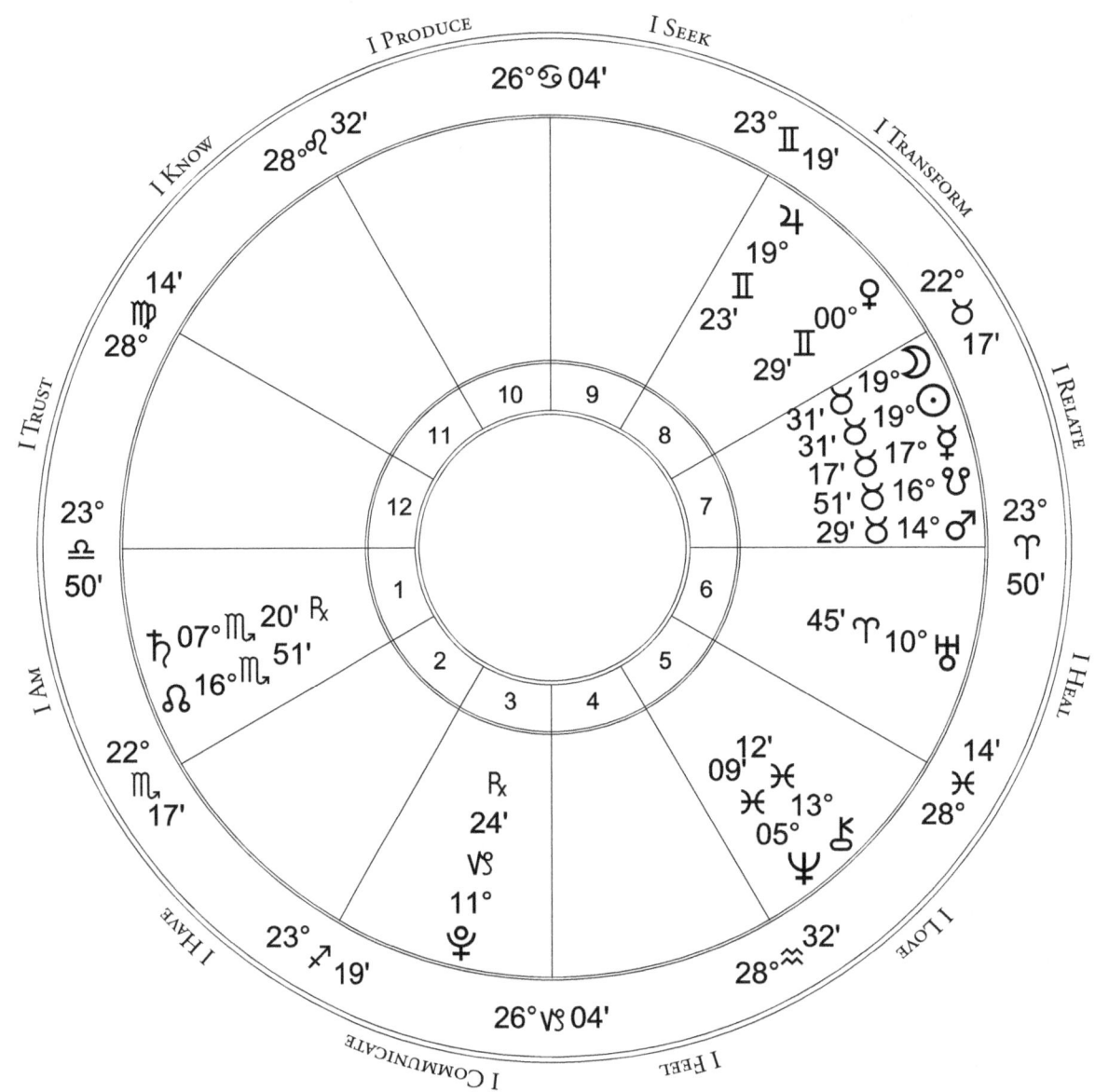

♈ Aries	♋ Cancer	♏ Scorpio	♓ Pisces	♀ Venus	♅ Uranus	☊ North Node
♉ Taurus	♌ Leo	♐ Sagittarius	☉ Sun	♂ Mars	♆ Neptune	☋ South Node
♊ Gemini	♍ Virgo	♑ Capricorn	☽ Moon	♃ Jupiter	♀ or ♇ Pluto	℞ Retrograde
	♎ Libra	♒ Aquarius	☿ Mercury	♄ Saturn	⚷ Chiron	

new Moon in Taurus

May 9, 5:29 PM – Solar Eclipse

Cosmic Check-In

Take a moment to write a brief phrase for each "I" statement.
This activates all areas of your life for this creative cycle.

♉ I Have

♊ I Communicate

♋ I Feel

♌ I Love

♍ I Heal

♎ I Relate

♏ I Transform

♐ I Seek

♑ I Produce

♒ I Know

♓ I Trust

♈ I Am

Full Moon in Sagittarius

May 24, 9:26 PM – Lunar Eclipse

Statement I Seek
Body Thighs
Mind Philosophical
Spirit Inspiration

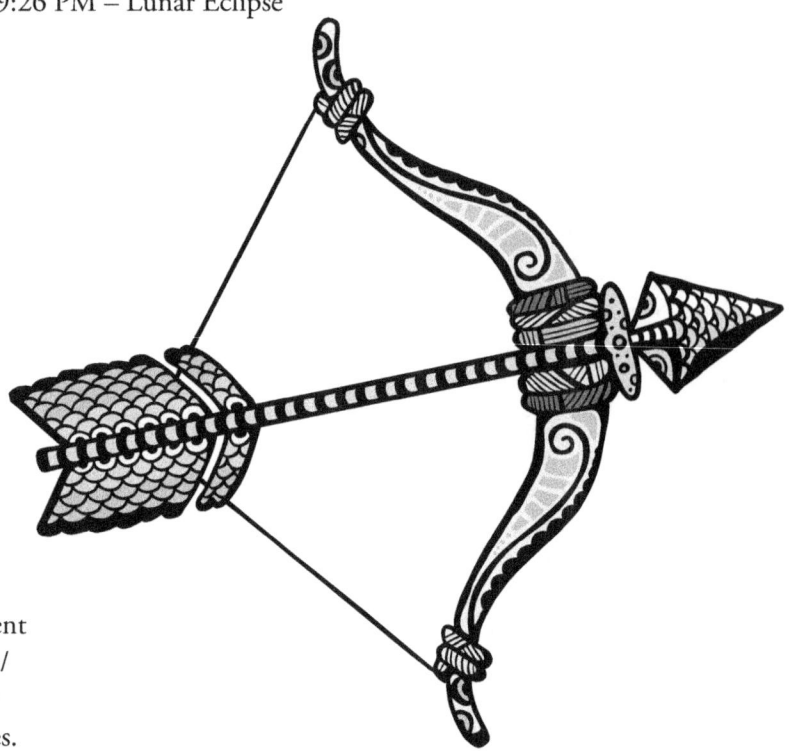

The Sun is Opposite the Moon

Full Moons are always in opposition to the Sun. This creates a feeling of tension between where you want to shine and how your feelings are flowing on a sensory level about the Sun's directive. The two forces seem like they are working against each other, yet they are on the same team displaying different techniques to attain the same mission. The Sagittarius/Gemini polarity creates tension between the quest for higher knowledge and the need for academic accolades.

Sagittarius Goddess

Iris, the Rainbow Goddess, is a symbol of multi-colored and multi-dimensional consciousness. She weaves many mysteries into the garment of life with her colors. The Rainbow Bridge gave Iris access to travel between Heaven and Earth. She was Hera's messenger bringing visions and messages for greater awareness to those who needed insight. For this reason, part of the eye was named after her. The Rainbow is a symbol of a fortunate future and reminds us that we have the potential to manifest in all spheres and circumstances. One of Iris' jobs is to cut the cord of life to those crossing over to the other side and open the directive for the pathway of light. When the Moon is full in Sagittarius, we may find ourselves lost or directionless. It is time to call on the power of Iris to bring a new vision.

Sagittarius Freedom List Ideas

Now is the time to free myself from…

- Belief systems that no longer apply
- Attitudes that are not uplifting to you
- Addiction to excess and risk
- The need to exaggerate based on low self-esteem
- Dishonest people
- Being too blunt
- Staying in the future and avoiding the NOW
- Overriding fear by being too optimistic
- Preaching

On Your Altar

Colors: Deep purple, turquoise, royal blue
Numerology: 9 – sing with joy in your heart
Tarot Card: Temperance – balancing the present with the past, updating yourself
Gemstone: Turquoise
Plant Remedy: Madia – seeing and hitting the target
Fragrance: Magnolia – expanded beauty

Full Moon in Sagittarius

May 24, 9:26 PM – Lunar Eclipse

Memory Maintenance Meditation

The Moon governs our memory and the maintenance of our memory. It is our memory that often creates blocks to setting us free to be able to attain our goals. The Moon works with us to help us become free from memory blocks three days after the Full Moon. The freedom themes are provided by the zodiac sign and can be from this lifetime or other lifetimes. These meditations assist in dissolving blocks and open pathways to new frontiers.

When the Moon is in Sagittarius, it is a time to become aware of dependency on rituals and philosophies. Look for perceptions of loyalty, fidelity, and ethics that keep you stuck in the past. Close your eyes and take in a few breaths. Ask for nighttime instructions from the Angel of Records to assist you in discovering a time when you became dependent on a practice that no longer serves you, your truth, your reality, and your daring. The Angel of Ritual will connect you to the new rituals that need to be reawakened at this time to empower your growth in the moment.

Sagittarius Challenges and Victories

Today I blend my old self with my new self, my physical reality with my spiritual awareness, my positive thoughts with my negative thoughts, my past with my present, my feminine with my masculine, my rewards with my losses, my ups and my downs, and my higher self with my lower self. It is a day for me to refine and fine tune my life by looking at my extremes. I recognize what inspires me and what keeps me stuck. I find my center today by acknowledging my extremes. I am aware that balance comes to those who are able to locate the space in the center of these opposite energy fields. When I am in my center my polarities are in motion. Healing cannot occur unless my polarities are moving and I know healing is motion.

I am ready for a healing today and know that by visiting my opposites and determining their vast opposition to each other I can find the paradoxes that I have chosen for myself and begin to heal. I am willing to experiment with this blending of opposites and become the alchemist of my own life. When I blend all aspects of myself rather than separating them, I can truly become whole. Today is a day to integrate, rather than separate, in order to release the spark of light that stays a prisoner when my polarities are in operation. When I find balance, motion occurs and the Law of Harmony takes over, putting paradoxical energies to rest, thus breaking the crystallization of polarity. The Law of Harmony is beauty in motion, promoting the flow of color, light, sound, and movement into form. Balance is a condition that keeps my spark in motion. I become the vertical line in the center of polarity today and carry the secret of balance. Balance cannot be my goal, motion my goal today. When I am in motion I can take action to evolve and to express all of myself freely.

Sagittarius Homework

Time to use your physical body to release the feeling of being caged in by people or circumstances. Choose an activity that burns away confinement and allows you to feel the power of your passion.

The Sagittarius Moon awakens us to know the spark of light that lives in our heart, thus elevating love in ourselves and in our world. This is when we come to realize what is in our highest and best good and we can begin to become free from all that is not lovable in our lives.

Full Moon in Sagittarius

May 24, 9:26 PM – Lunar Eclipse

Five Steps to Freedom

When we work with the concept of freedom we are soon presented with resistance. Freedom presents a pathway for us to bump directly into our limitations. When we can become aware of these limits, we can then find our way to freedom. Below are some ideas that might assist you in seeing deeper into your resistance to accepting freedom into your life. Once you discover these you might want to add more to your freedom list.

1. Feeling Useless

This happens when you measure yourself by what others think of you.

2. Discouragement

This occurs when you use blame others instead of taking responsibility for your part in a situation.

3. Regret

This happens when you live inside past events and continue to rehearse your story, hoping that if you tell it enough, it will get resolved. Living in the past leads to regret and blocks you from freedom.

4. Limitation

This happens when we think that there is no way out of a challenge, which creates an inability to see options. When options are out of the picture we become unable to create positive outcomes.

5. Self-Doubt

This takes place when we think that others are better than we are. Growing cannot occur when we have given someone else our ceiling.

Full Moon in Sagittarius

May 24, 9:26 PM – Lunar Eclipse

My Freedom List

Sagittarius Questions to Ask Myself

How can I refresh my agreement with life?

How can I be an inspiration without interfering?

What do I need to do to re-translate honesty into trueness into my life?

Full Moon in Sagittarius

May 24, 9:26 PM – Lunar Eclipse

How to Use Your Chart with the Moon Book

Begin by looking for the Moon icon on the chart below. Directly below the Moon icon is a number written in bold type. That number is the degree of the Full Moon on this day. Find 07° Leo on your own chart and look for the theme, written on the outside of the astro-wheel, to see how this Moon will work for you. This theme will help to set the tone for your Freedom List.

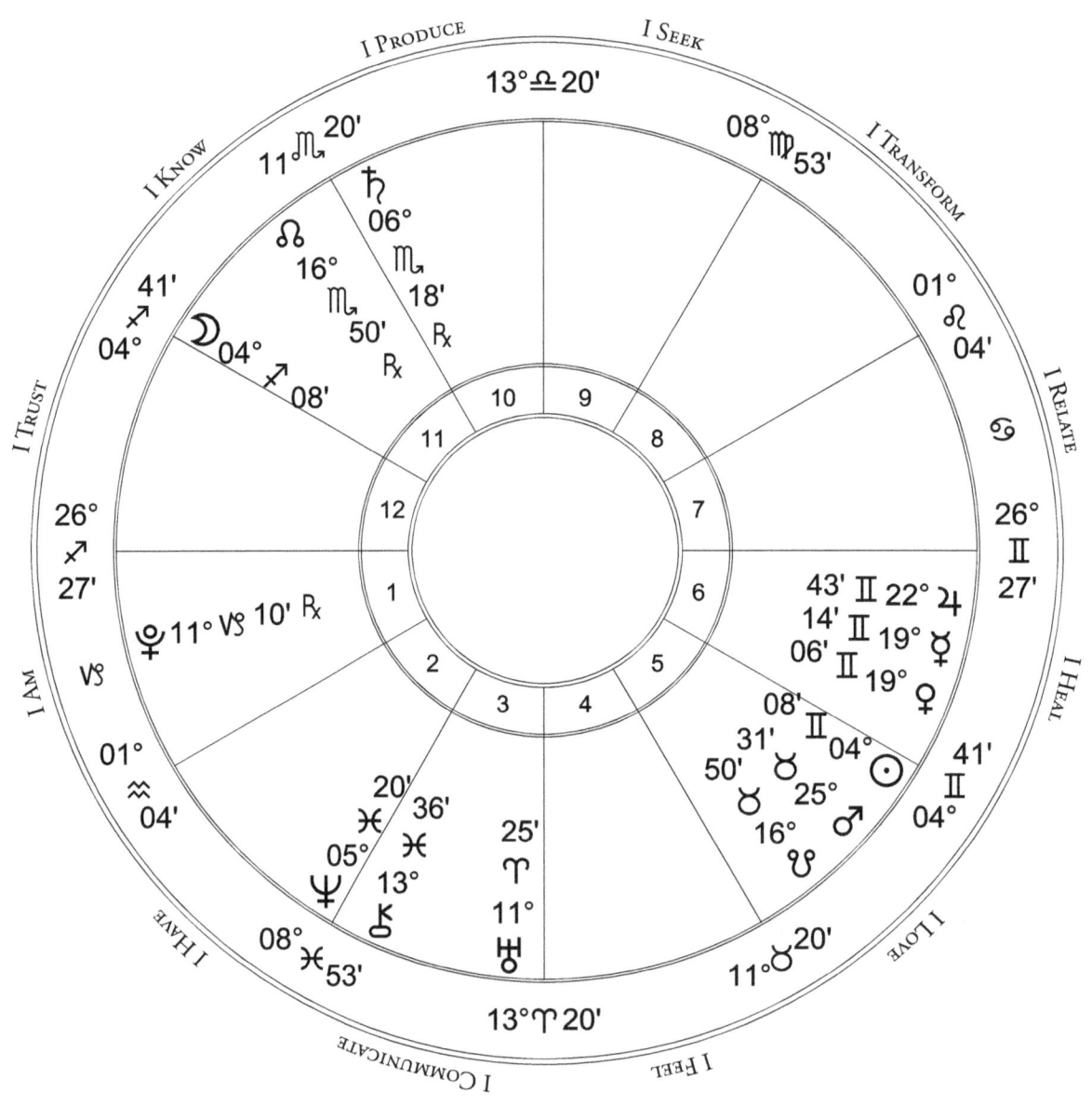

♈ Aries	♋ Cancer	♏ Scorpio	♓ Pisces	♀ Venus	♅ Uranus	☊ North Node
♉ Taurus	♌ Leo	♐ Sagittarius	☉ Sun	♂ Mars	♆ Neptune	☋ South Node
♊ Gemini	♍ Virgo	♑ Capricorn	☽ Moon	♃ Jupiter	♀ or ♇ Pluto	℞ Retrograde
	♎ Libra	♒ Aquarius	☿ Mercury	♄ Saturn	⚷ Chiron	

Full Moon in Sagittarius

May 24, 9:26 PM – Lunar Eclipse

Cosmic Check-In

Take a moment to write a brief phrase for each "I" statement.
This activates all areas of your life for this freedom cycle.

♐ I Seek

♑ I Produce

♒ I Know

♓ I Trust

♈ I Am

♉ I Have

♊ I Communicate

♋ I Feel

♌ I Love

♍ I Heal

♎ I Relate

♏ I Transform

June 2013

SUN	MON	TUE	WED	THU	FRI	SAT
						1 ♄♀℞ ☽ V/C 9:31 PM ☽ → ♈ 11:35 AM 8. Your abundance helps others.
2 ♄♀℞ ♀ → ♋ 7:14 PM 9. Respect the temple of your body.	**3** ♄♀℞ ☽ V/C 11:10 PM 10. If you feel stuck, start over.	**4** ♄♀℞ ☽ → ♉ 8:54 AM 11. You are much more than you know.	**5** ♄♀℞ ☽ V/C 6:26 AM 3. Let your belief system continue to evolve.	**6** ♄♀℞ ☽ → ♊ 8:33 PM 4. You have all the tools you need.	**7** ♄♀♆℞ ♆℞—5°♓22′ 1:25 AM 5. At all times, change is your friend.	**8** ♄♀♆℞ ▼ 18°♊01′ 8:57 AM 6. Respect the sacred space of your home.
9 ♄♀♆℞ ▼ ☽ V/C 1:30 AM ☽ → ♋ 9:17 AM 7. What would you like to learn about?	**10** ♄♀♆℞ ☽ V/C 2:16 PM 8. Use your success to help others.	**11** ♄♀♆℞ ☽ → ♌ 9:59 PM 9. Inspire others by your good example.	**12** ♄♀♆℞ 10. Take action to fulfill your dreams.	**13** ♄♀♆℞ 11. All is well in all of creation.	**14** ♄♀♆℞ Flag Day ☽ V/C 4:15 AM ☽ → ♍ 9:27 AM 3. Worry is a total waste of time.	**15** ♄♀♆℞ 4. Find the structure that works best.
16 ♄♀♆⚷℞ Father's Day ⚷℞ ♓ 2:18 AM ☽ V/C 2:27 PM ☽ → ♎ 6:20 PM 5. Celebrate the liberation of change.	**17** ♄♀♆⚷℞ 6. Acquire something beautiful for your home.	**18** ♄♀♆⚷℞ ☽ V/C 8:56 PM ☽ → ♏ 11:39 PM 7. Do not be inhibited by your mind.	**19** ♄♀♆⚷℞ 8. Abundance is related to your desire to live.	**20** ♄♀♆⚷℞ Summer Solstice ☽ V/C 12:16 PM ☉ → ♋ 10:05 PM 9. Stand centered in prayer.	**21** ♄♀♆⚷℞ ▲ ☽ → ♐ 1:32 AM 10. Consider traveling to a new place.	**22** ♄♀♆⚷℞ ▲ 11. The Universe has no limits.
23 ♄♀♆⚷℞ 02°♑10′ 4:33 AM V/C 12:09 AM ☽ → ♑ 1:09 AM 3. Find joy in doing simple things.	**24** ♄♀♆⚷℞ ☽ V/C 7:25 PM 4. Honor your commitments.	**25** ♄♀♆⚷℞ ☽ → ♒ 12:28 AM ♃ → ♋ 6:41 PM 5. Find a new approach that works.	**26** ☿♄♀♆⚷℞ ☽ V/C 6:09 AM ☿℞—23°♋0′ 6:09AM 6. Invite friends for dinner tonight.	**27** ☿♄♀♆⚷ ☽ → ♓ 1:33 AM ♀ → ♌ 10:04 AM 7. Be open to new learning.	**28** ☿♄♀♆⚷℞ ☽ V/C 5:17 PM 8. Find satisfaction in what you do.	**29** ☿♄♀♆⚷℞ ☽ → ♈ 6:08 AM 9. Donate to a humanitarian cause.
30 ☿♄♀♆⚷℞ ☽ V/C 11:49 PM 10. Take a positive step into the future.						

June 2013 Planetary Highlights

Saturn Continues to be Retrograde in Scorpio all Month

Look inward and see how your mind determines its course to sequester your ideas rather than sharing them. Find out how this inner working in you establishes secrets and mystery to give you a false sense of power. Then, make a realization about how much energy gets used up doing this and begin to transform and share your thoughts.

Pluto Continues to be Retrograde in Capricorn all Month

Take a good look at your relationship with money. Get to know your reaction to receiving it, making it, saving it, giving it, sharing it, and spending it. Impulse and unpredictability can play havoc with your relationship with money and bring a mixed bag of tricks for fortune and misfortune. A proper understanding between your heart and your bank account is necessary in order to receive the gifts that are available this month.

June 7, 1:27AM – Neptune goes retrograde in Pisces

Expect clouded vision veiling you from your truth and your truth where others are concerned. Pay attention to where you have displaced your feelings. Ask your ego to gently open the flood gates so you can deal with any distortions. Neptune retrograde asks us to face our disappointments and get real.

June 8 and June 23 – Venus and Mercury are coupled in Cancer

Re-vamp your home so that it communicates who you are.

June 16, 2:18 AM – Chiron goes Retrograde in Pisces

Allow yourself to bump close up to your feelings and let the healing waters of Pisces wash them away.

June 20, 10:05 PM – The Sun enters Cancer

Happy Summer Solstice! This is the peak of the growing season and it is time to ask yourself, "How is my personal garden growing?" Make a list of what you have planted so far this year and see what still needs a little fertilizer.

June 23 – Jupiter in Gemini and the Sun in Cancer Conjunct Opposing the Full Moon in Capricorn

The Sun is on the balance point between public life versus personal life. An enormous amount of radiance will be activating a major integration of happiness for both ends of the balance point. Celebrate and communicate the best of both worlds.

June 25 6:41 PM – Jupiter enters Cancer

We can expect many blessings for our home and family with an increase of abundance and nurturing. Expect good feelings to flow, bringing about a higher heart expression in relationships. This will bring good fortune to real estate and all businesses connected to home building and interior design and to all home-related services. This increase will come with Jupiter's extravagance as well, so make sure you don't go into overflow.

June 26, 6:09 AM – Mercury goes Retrograde in Cancer

Think twice before speaking especially with family members. Reactions from past misunderstanding can happen and make it hard to hear correctly. A good thing to remember at this time are Buddha's words regarding speaking. Ask yourself, "Is it kind?" "Is it truthful?" "Is it necessary?"

June 27, 6:41 AM – Venus enters Leo

It's party time! This sets the tone for fun and creativity to become part of our summer. Love life expresses itself in rewarding ways by actually living the romantic way, rather than imagining it. Expect to do a lot of shopping and know that generosity is part of the abundance you feel. Enjoy!

June 21 and 22 – Super-Sensitivity ▲

Worry and fear can hook you up to the chaos in the global consciousness. Do your best to avoid it!

June 8 and 9 – Low-Vitality ▼

Be willing to flow with the tides of change in order to stay energized at this time. Remember resistance leads to exhaustion.

♈ Aries	♋ Cancer	♐ Sagittarius	☽ Moon	♄ Saturn	☊ North Node	V/C Void-of-Course
♉ Taurus	♌ Leo	♑ Capricorn	☿ Mercury	♅ Uranus	☋ South Node	▲ Super-Sensitivity
♊ Gemini	♍ Virgo	♒ Aquarius	♀ Venus	♆ Neptune	➡ Enters	▼ Low-Vitality
	♎ Libra	♓ Picses	♂ Mars	♀ or ♇ Pluto	℞ Retrograde	
	♏ Scorpio	☉ Sun	♃ Jupiter	⚷ Chiron	S/D Stationary Direct	

New Moon in Gemini

June 8, 8:57 AM

Statement I Communicate
Body Lungs and Hands
Mind Intellect
Spirit Intelligence

When the Sun is in Gemini

This is a time when the ability to communicate is at the top of the priority list. Allow your thoughts to lead you to a formula for success so you can put your thoughts into action. Then, find the appropriate soapbox to stand on so your message can be heard. Right now is the time to make your message clear, enlightening, witty, and thought-provoking. Your bright mind is at its high throne and waiting for an audience. Try blogging, do a show on YouTube, join Toast Masters, write that screenplay, film yourself doing a travel show, start a discussion group, or write a newsletter for your neighborhood. Most of all, put your bright mind to work!

Gemini Co-Creation Ideas

Now is the time to focus on...

- Communications
- Promotion
- Technology
- Ideas
- Non-judgmental communication
- Thinking outside of duality
- A quiet mind
- Charisma and charm
- Flirting

Gemini Goddess

Maya is the goddess of illusion. She tempts the mind into believing that what it thinks is always correct. She challenges you every step of the way to learn where the ego kicks in and leads you down pathways that are destructive. Her constant "mind chatter" sounds so convincing that one can spend an entire life living the illusion that thinking is better than experiencing. Maya will build this illusion so deep in the mind that you actually believe that your thoughts are worthy of accolades in the outer world. She distorts the value of inner work to keep you from knowing your personal truth.

On Your Altar

Colors: Bright yellow, orange, multi-colors

Numerology: 6 – respect your private space at home

Tarot Card: Lovers – connecting to wholeness

Gemstones: Yellow diamond, citrine

Plant Remedy: Morning Glory – thinking with your heart not your head

Fragrance: Iris – the ability to focus the mind

new Moon in Gemini

June 8, 8:57 AM

Gemini Challenges and Victories

I am dark. I am light. I am day. I am night. The extremes in life exist within me, completing themselves in reality. The "I" that is "we" lives within me. I am one in the same. I am both.

I know that flow comes from accepting my opposite natures. Today, I accept my opposites and get into the flow. I am aware today of how my judgments separate me from people, events, experiences, and, most of all, from myself. Today I am going to see where I have separated all of the parts of myself and begin to integrate into wholeness through acceptance and understanding. I begin by breathing. I breathe in wholeness and breathe out separation. I understand that breath is life and that life includes all facets of my experience to gain awareness. I know that I am Heaven. I know that I am Earth. I know that I am masculine. I know that I am feminine. Today, I become unified. Today, I integrate into wholeness. I breathe into all of these aspects of myself, knowing that in my totality I am connected to Oneness. The "I" that is "we" lives within me. I am one in the same. I am both.

Gemini Homework

The Gemini co-creates best through broadcasting and journalism, as a speech coach, comedian, political satirist, gossip columnist, negotiator, media specialist, manicurist, salesperson, teacher, or travel consultant.

Expect to awaken your will on seven levels…

- The will to direct through the power of your original intention.
- The will to love stimulating goodwill among humankind through cooperation.
- The will to take action by laying foundations for a happier world.
- The will to cooperate the desire and demand for right relationships.
- The will to know how to think correctly and creatively so that every man/woman can find their outstanding characteristic.
- The will to persist to be one with your light and represent the ideal standard for living.
- The will to organize to carry forward direct inspiration through groups of goodwill.

New Moon in Gemini

June 8, 8:57 AM

Five Steps to Co-Creation

1. Acceptance

Acceptance opens the pathway to living in the moment and makes way for opportunity to occur. Co-creation can only occur when you live in the moment.

Start your list by writing… "I accept _____ into my life."

2. Adjustment

Consider what adjustments you may need to make in order to receive what you are accepting into your life.

My Co-Creation List

New Moon in Gemini

June 8, 8:57 AM

3. Awakening

Once your list is complete, use the power of sound and read your list out loud. This directs your intentions (your list) toward actualization and co-creation.

4. Alignment

Now it is time to make a petition to the Universe, using these words, "I call on the power of the Universe to know I am ready to receive my list. I accept it. I allow it. So be it! This, or something better than this, comes to me in an easy and pleasurable way for the good of all concerned. Thank You Universe!" Light your candle and place it on your eight-sided mirror.

5. Acknowledgement

When a creation result is acknowledged it seals the deal. This makes room for more magnificence to expand into your life and increases your abundance factor adding to your ability to receive.

As each aspect of your co-creation list arrives in your life, spend time allowing, acknowledging, and accepting it with the true gusto of gratitude. You might want to make a victory list here.

Victory List

Gemini Questions to ask Myself

Where do I go against my intuition and use my ego mind to make decisions?

How can I live making split-second choices based on the truth of the moment?

What do I need to do to turn over dominion to my Soul and not be threatened by external forces?

new Moon in Gemini

June 8, 8:57 AM

How to Use the Moon Book With Your Chart

Fill in the blanks on the Cosmic Check-In page. Then look up the degree of the moon on the chart below. Take note of the "I" statement on the outside of the wheel where the moon is located. Now locate the same degree on your own chart, and make a note of the house and corresponding "I" statement. Go back to the Cosmic Check-In page and circle the two statements from the charts and read what you wrote. This will give you an idea about what to expect from this moon phase on a personal level.

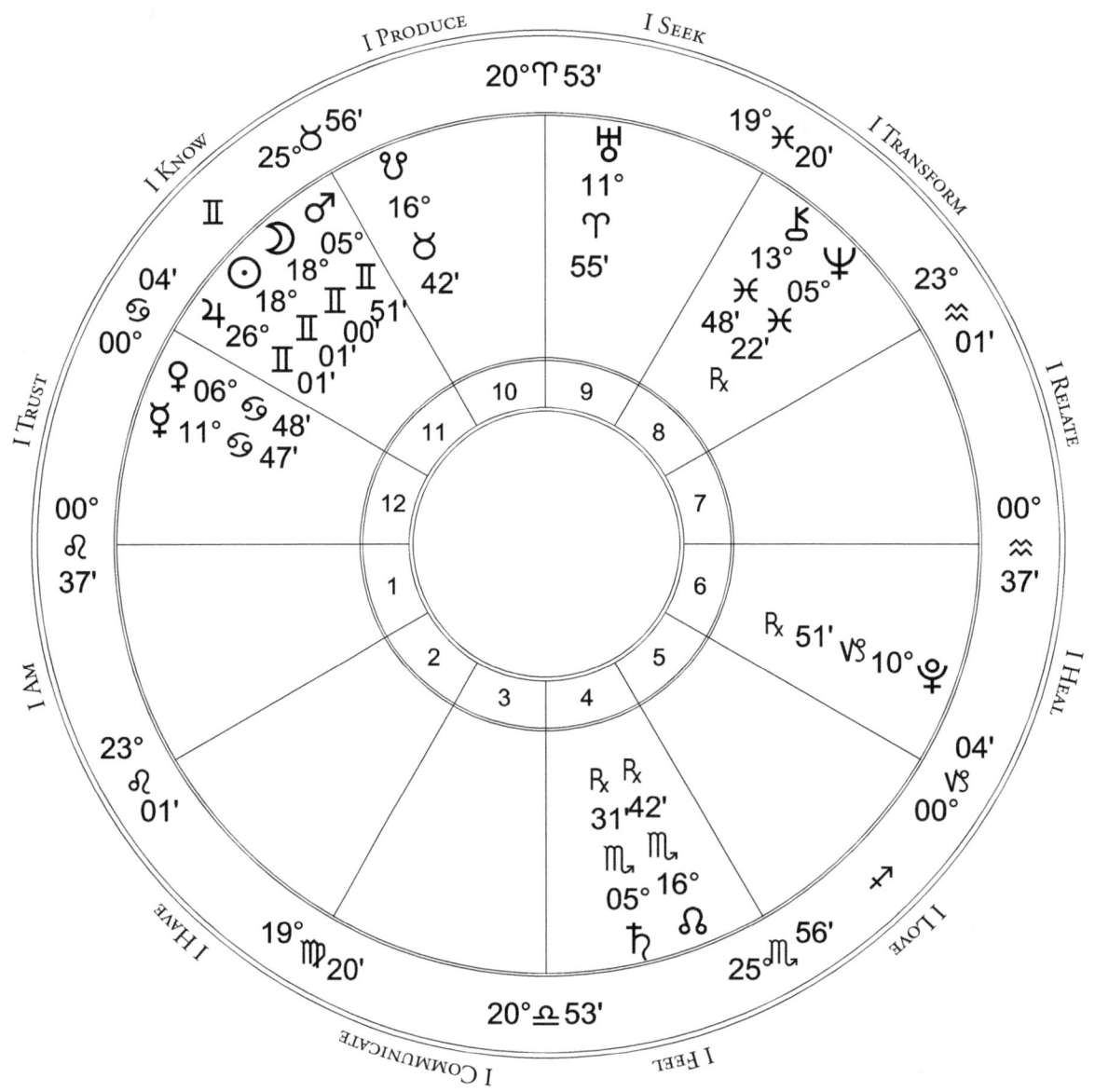

♈ Aries	♋ Cancer	♏ Scorpio	♓ Pisces	♀ Venus	♅ Uranus	☊ North Node
♉ Taurus	♌ Leo	♐ Sagittarius	☉ Sun	♂ Mars	♆ Neptune	☋ South Node
♊ Gemini	♍ Virgo	♑ Capricorn	☽ Moon	♃ Jupiter	♀ or ♇ Pluto	℞ Retrograde
	♎ Libra	♒ Aquarius	☿ Mercury	♄ Saturn	⚷ Chiron	

new Moon in Gemini

June 8, 8:57 AM

Cosmic Check-In

Take a moment to write a brief phrase for each "I" statement.
This activates all areas of your life for this creative cycle.

♊ I Communicate

♋ I Feel

♌ I Love

♍ I Heal

♎ I Relate

♏ I Transform

♐ I Seek

♑ I Produce

♒ I Know

♓ I Trust

♈ I Am

♉ I Have

Full Moon in Capricorn

June 23, 4:33 AM

Statement I Produce
Body Knees
Mind Authority Issues
Spirit Advance Civilization

The Sun is Opposite the Moon

Full Moons are always in opposition to the Sun. This creates a feeling of tension between where you want to shine and how your feelings are flowing on a sensory level about the Sun's directive. The two forces seem like they are working against each other, yet they are on the same team displaying different techniques to attain the same mission. The Capricorn/Cancer polarity creates tension between the quest for status and the need to feel secure.

Capricorn Goddess

Capricorn goddess, Kali, stands guard with her sword ready to slice away our demons of ignorance and resistance so we can move into our rightful position. She cuts away delusion and denial to assist us in creating beyond the limitations of our mind. Kali reminds us that every experience is an invitation to wake up. She will fight with us every step of the way until we accept our authority with integrity. When we accept her power and embrace Kali, our problems dissolve and we experience radiant bliss, freedom from limitation of the mind, and right use of our power.

Capricorn Freedom List Ideas

Now is the time to free myself from…

- Obstacles to success
- Authority issues
- Sorrow and sadness
- Fear that blocks you
- Arrogance and irritability
- Limitations of time
- Priorities that are no longer valid
- Control and domination
- The need to do it all alone
- Responsibility

On Your Altar

Colors: Forest green, earth tones

Numerology: 3 – take time out to be social

Tarot Card: Devil – confinement, attachment to form, look at the broader view

Gemstones: Smoky quartz, topaz, garnet

Plant Remedy: Rosemary – activates appropriate memory

Fragrance: Frankincense – assists the Soul's entry into the body

Full Moon in Capricorn

June 23, 4:33 AM

Memory Maintenance Meditation

The Moon governs our memory and the maintenance of our memory. It is our memory that often creates blocks to setting us free to be able to attain our goals. The Moon works with us to help us become free from memory blocks three days after the Full Moon. The freedom themes are provided by the zodiac sign and can be from this lifetime or other lifetimes. These meditations assist in dissolving blocks and open pathways to new frontiers.

Begin by sitting down in a comfortable position, close your eyes and breathe in and out while asking for the Angel of Humility to show you the kernel of the heart of humility. Begin by releasing arrogance. Review the force of your thrusting will to determine the quality of your executive power. Release irritability and self-reproach. Renew the concept of true devotion and dedicate yourself to the Divine master plan of the Universe. This will set you free.

Capricorn Challenges and Victories

I feel limited. I feel confined. I feel stuck. I feel there is no way out. Perhaps I am the target of someone's envy or jealousy, or perhaps I am jealous or I am envious. Maybe I am spending too much time in the outer world and putting too much value on material rewards, things, and possessions. Maybe I am trying to possess someone or limit their view or choice. I may feel there are no choices. Maybe I am living by someone else's rules and beliefs and forgot how to think for myself. I could also be overcome by fear and too terrorized to look at anything at all.

Today, I see and feel the limits of placing the source of love outside myself. I have tunnel vision and I seem to have forgotten to look at my options. I must ask myself today, "How many ways can I look at my life, my situation, or my perceived problems?" Today I must expand my view to encompass 360° instead of only 180°. I begin by acknowledging to myself that today is the worst it is going to get. I know deep within me that if I allow myself to truly experience my bottom, the top will become visible to me. It is time to look at the brighter side.

Begin by identifying the problem by writing it down on a piece of paper. Start with the phrase, "The problem is_____." Fill in the blanks. Then, list as many solutions to the problem as you can. List at least three. Then, say these solutions out loud every day until the answer comes to you through a person, an idea, an event, or a choice.

Capricorn Homework

Put on a good pair of walking shoes and get ready to walk your blues away. It is time to get outside and feel the loving power of mother earth. The green of the trees refreshes your stagnant energy while you exhaust yourself to a point of vulnerability. Then, and only then, will you feel freedom. Give yourself permission to throw your watch away and learn to live in the moment.

The Capricorn moon is the reincarnation of Spirit emerging from the dark waters of our past emotions and releasing us from our fear of change and our fear of loss. Awaken your powerful and positive spiritual connection to be open to new possibilities. Ask yourself to release your emotional loyalty to the past. We are reminded of our need for material and emotional security at this time. In order to ensure this, we must learn to build a foundation for ourselves that is lit from within, made from the materials of love, goodwill, and intelligence.

Full Moon in Capricorn

June 23, 4:33 AM

Five Steps to Freedom

When we work with the concept of freedom we are soon presented with resistance. Freedom presents a pathway for us to bump directly into our limitations. When we can become aware of these limits, we can then find our way to freedom. Below are some ideas that might assist you in seeing deeper into your resistance to accepting freedom into your life. Once you discover these you might want to add more to your freedom list.

1. Feeling Useless

This happens when you measure yourself by what others think of you.

2. Discouragement

This occurs when you use blame others instead of taking responsibility for your part in a situation.

3. Regret

This happens when you live inside past events and continue to rehearse your story, hoping that if you tell it enough, it will get resolved. Living in the past leads to regret and blocks you from freedom.

4. Limitation

This happens when we think that there is no way out of a challenge, which creates an inability to see options. When options are out of the picture we become unable to create positive outcomes.

5. Self-Doubt

This takes place when we think that others are better than we are. Growing cannot occur when we have given someone else our ceiling.

full Moon in Capricorn
June 23, 4:33 AM

My Freedom List

Capricorn Questions to Ask Myself

Where do I let my fear of change stop me from receiving my spiritual inheritance?

Do I make my choices based on anxiety and fear or on my highest potential?

How can I build the tools within me for holding the space to build my individuality and my collective consciousness at the same time?

Full Moon in Capricorn

June 23, 4:33 AM

How to Use the Moon Book With Your Chart

Fill in the blanks on the Cosmic Check-In page. Then look up the degree of the moon on the chart below. Take note of the "I" statement on the outside of the wheel where the moon is located. Now locate the same degree on your own chart, and make a note of the house and corresponding "I" statement. Go back to the Cosmic Check-In page and circle the two statements from the charts and read what you wrote. This will give you an idea about what to expect from this moon phase on a personal level.

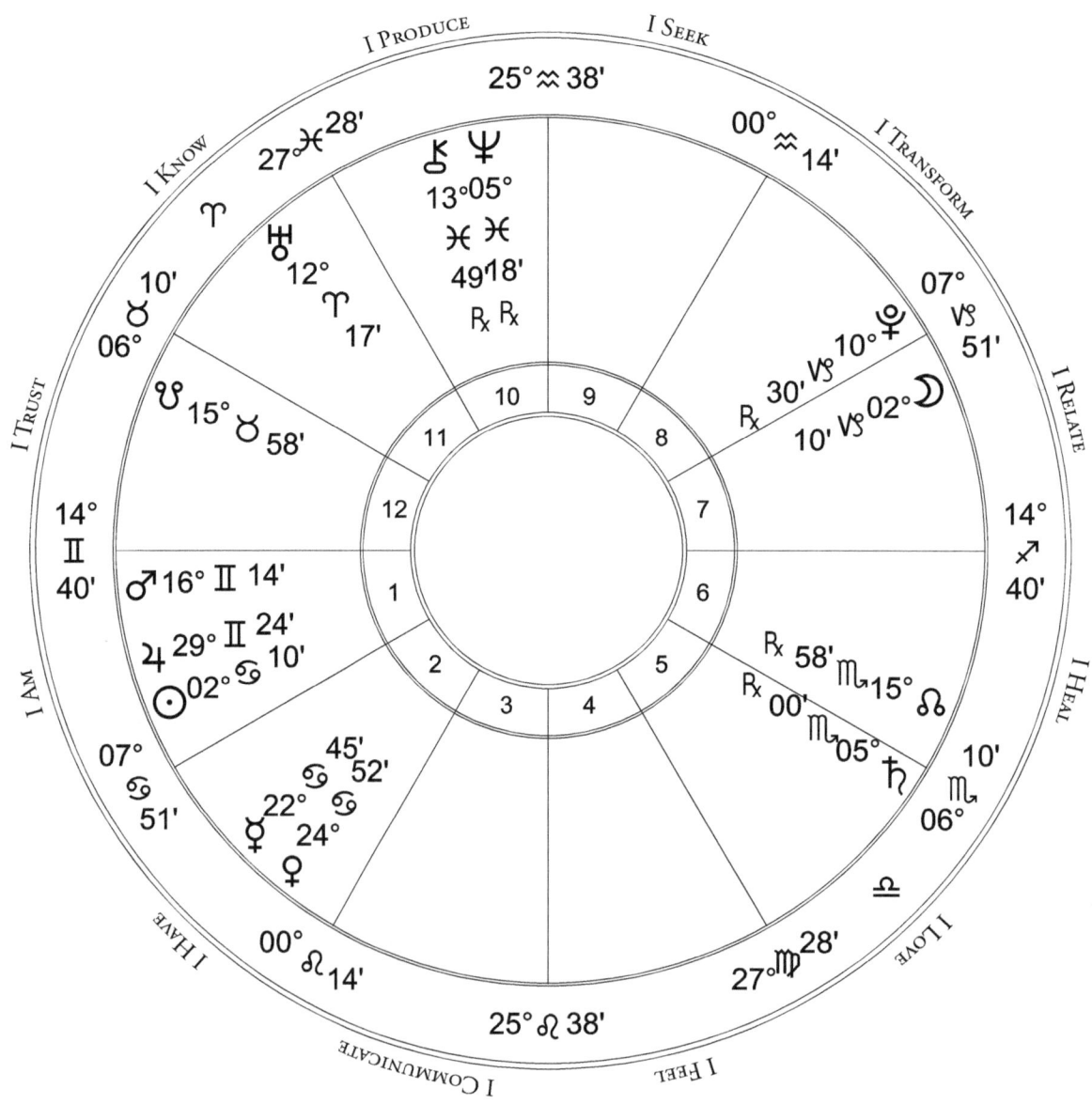

♈ Aries	♋ Cancer	♏ Scorpio	♓ Pisces	♀ Venus	♅ Uranus	☊ North Node
♉ Taurus	♌ Leo	♐ Sagittarius	☉ Sun	♂ Mars	♆ Neptune	☋ South Node
♊ Gemini	♍ Virgo	♑ Capricorn	☽ Moon	♃ Jupiter	♀ or ♇ Pluto	℞ Retrograde
	♎ Libra	♒ Aquarius	☿ Mercury	♄ Saturn	⚷ Chiron	

116

full Moon in Capricorn

June 23, 4:33 AM

Cosmic Check-In

Take a moment to write a brief phrase for each "I" statement.
This activates all areas of your life for this freedom cycle.

♑ I Produce

♒ I Know

♓ I Trust

♈ I Am

♉ I Have

♊ I Communicate

♋ I Feel

♌ I Love

♍ I Heal

♎ I Relate

♏ I Transform

♐ I Seek

117

July 2013

SUN	MON	TUE	WED	THU	FRI	SAT
	1 ☿♄♀♆⚷℞ ☽ → ♉ 2:44 PM 11. You are an important part of the Universe.	**2** ☿♄♀♆⚷℞ 3. Do something fun today.	**3** ☿♄♀♆⚷℞ ☽ V/C 8:52 AM 4. At all times, stand in your integrity.	**4** ☿♄♀♆⚷℞ Independence Day ☽ → ♊ 2:22 AM 5. Take a walk on a new path.	**5** ☿♄♀♆⚷℞▼ 6. See your home as your castle.	**6** ☿♄♀♆⚷℞▼ ☽ V/C 5:31 AM ☽ → ♋ 3:15 PM 7. Take credit for what you know.
7 ☿♀♆⚷℞ ♄ SD 4°♏49′ 10:13 PM 8. Make every negotiation a win-win situation.	**8** ☿♀♆⚷℞ ● 16°♋18′ 12:15 AM ☽ V/C 4:45 AM 9. Support causes that improve humanity.	**9** ☿♀♆⚷℞ ☽ → ♌ 3:49 AM 10. See yourself evolving.	**10** ☿♀♆⚷℞ 2. After you deliberate, take action.	**11** ☿♀♆⚷℞ ☽ V/C 12:55 PM ☽ → ♍ 3:13 PM 3. Worrying is a waste of energy.	**12** ☿♀♆⚷℞ 4. Stay loyal to your intention.	**13** ☿♀♆⚷℞ ♂ → ♋ 6:23 AM ☽ V/C 8:27 AM 5. Commit to exercising daily.
14 ☿♀♆⚷℞ ☽ → ♎ 12:42 AM 6. Is it time for a physical checkup?	**15** ☿♀♆⚷℞ ☽ V/C 8:17 PM 7. Don't confuse thinking with thought.	**16** ☿♀♆⚷℞ ☽ → ♏ 7:25 AM 8. Abundance flows with action.	**17** ☿♀♆♅⚷℞ ♅℞ 12°♈31′ 10:21 AM 9. Pray for our highest and best good.	**18** ☿♀♆♅⚷℞ ☽ V/C 4:13 AM ☽ → ♐ 10:55 AM 10. Be inspired by something new.	**19** ☿♀♆♅⚷℞▲ 2. Look at both sides of every issue.	**20** ♀♆♅⚷℞▲ ☽ V/C 8:01 AM ☿D 13°♋21′ 11:23 AM ☽ → ♑ 11:40 AM 3. Complaining perpetrates the problem.
21 ♀♆♅⚷℞ ☽ V/C 8:54 AM 4. Clear out obsolete files.	**22** ♀♆♅⚷ ○ 0°♒06′ 11:17 AM ♀ → ♍ 5:42 AM ☉ → ♌ 8:57 AM ☽ → ♒ 11:08 AM 5. When you are tired, slow down.	**23** ♀♆♅⚷℞ ☽ V/C 7:02 AM 6. Friendship is a two-way street.	**24** ♀♆♅⚷℞ ☽ → ♓ 11:23 AM 7. Ask advice from an expert.	**25** ♀♆♅⚷℞ ☽ V/C 11:44 AM 8. A good leader knows how to follow.	**26** ♀♆♅⚷℞ ☽ → ♈ 2:30 PM 9. Be a helping hand when needed.	**27** ♀♆♅⚷℞ ☽ V/C 7:20 PM 10. It's never too late to begin again.
28 ♀♆♅⚷℞ ☽ → ♉ 9:44 PM 2. Make decisions to take action.	**29** ♀♆♅⚷℞ 3. Find the humor in challenging situations.	**30** ♀♆♅⚷℞ ☽ V/C 8:59 AM 4. Staying flexible is an advantage.	**31** ♀♆♅⚷℞ ☽ → ♊ 8:43 AM 5. Do not push beyond your limits.			

July 2013 Planetary Highlights

Mercury is Retrograde in Cancer until July 20

Keep your finger on the hold button and stay in review mode. Review topics will relate to woman's issues, your home, and family. Personal nurturing programs such as make-overs and retreats that refresh your body are a very good idea for this time period. Please avoid signing any papers regarding new projects.

Saturn is Retrograde in Scorpio until July 7

So far this year, Saturn has confronted us with fears of loss, abandonment, powerlessness, and betrayal. It is now time to focus on what is left and how we can make the best of it without feeling the need to use control dramas on yourself or others. Questions to ask yourself, "How can I transform and heal from this perceived loss?" "How can I direct my energy band toward new events that do not involve controlling others?"

Pluto Retrograde in Capricorn for the Entire Month

It's time to check into our emotional loyalty to the past. See what strings are holding us there and bring restriction into our experience. Now is the time to become free from the old guard however that plays out for you.

Neptune Retrograde in Pisces all Month

There's always a risk of drifting off course with Neptune. Look at where you drifted off course and allowed a dream to dissolve inside your distraction. Instead of suffering over the loss, look at where you gave up, accept this, and acknowledge that you gave up. If you feel you want to re-kindle the dream, face it and start with whatever you've been putting off. (Hint: it will involve letting go of an established structure.) When Neptune is retrograde we must learn the difference between giving up and letting go.

July 17 – Uranus goes retrograde in Aries

Looking out for number one is the theme here. This will give us a chance to see where we sell out and bet on a goal that may or may not be good for our true identity.

July 13, 6:23 AM – Mars enters Cancer

Expect steam to come up and show you where you need to iron the wrinkles out of your old feelings. Lots of energy will come in to the family issues and home life. Accept this as a healing for all concerned and let it all come out. You may experience a sudden need to move, remodel, or, rearrange your furniture. Expect the home front to crave a makeover.

July 22, 5:42 AM – Venus enters Virgo

Image management comes to the foreground of our experience with this transit. Work on being kind to yourself when upgrading your appearance. Don't be too critical and ruin the fun.

July 22, 8:57 AM – The Sun enters Leo

It's party time! Spend time with friends and shine with confidence.

July 29-August 3 – The Grand Sextile

A six-pointed star made of two triangles, one pointing down and one pointing up, with different planets at each end. Seven planets are involved, all in earth and water elements of the feminine. This blessing comes straight from the heavens, advances the feminine, and brings a long-awaited grace to balance and heal the political, ecological, and social orders. It is known as the Saving Grace Sextile. It consists of 6 sextiles, 6 trines, and 3 oppositions. The healing trine involves the Moon, Venus, and Pluto, then Mars, Jupiter, Saturn, and Neptune all in earth and water. The engines that activate aliveness of this sextile are the oppositions with Mars/Jupiter opposite Pluto, the Moon opposite Saturn, and Venus opposite Neptune.

July 19 and 20 – Super-Sensitivity ▲

Avoid getting into too much thought right now. Take time out from anything that will put you into Chaos.

July 5 and 6 – Low-Vitality ▼

Pay special attention to the element of water—make sure you are drinking enough and work with letting your feelings flow to stay in balance.

♈ Aries	♋ Cancer	♐ Sagittarius	☽ Moon	♄ Saturn	☊ North Node	V/C Void-of-Course
♉ Taurus	♌ Leo	♑ Capricorn	☿ Mercury	♅ Uranus	☋ South Node	▲ Super-Sensitivity
♊ Gemini	♍ Virgo	♒ Aquarius	♀ Venus	♆ Neptune	→ Enters	▼ Low-Vitality
	♎ Libra	♓ Pisces	♂ Mars	♇ or ♇ Pluto	℞ Retrograde	
	♏ Scorpio	☉ Sun	♃ Jupiter	⚷ Chiron	S/D Stationary Direct	

New Moon in Cancer

July 8, 12:15 AM

Statement I Feel
Body Breasts
Mind Nurturing
Spirit Creator of Form

When the Sun is in Cancer

It is now time to build our structure and foundation. Cancer holds the wisdom of the Great Cosmic Architect. Her statement is, "I build a lighted house and therein I dwell." The key is to use the materials of light, love, and wisdom to build your house and become the creator of form. Look within to see what lights your home and your body. Also check security systems, early environmental training, and mother/child relationships to see what materials you are using to build the structure for your life. Use this creating Moon to build the structure you want.

Cancer Goddess

Birds are the symbol of expanded consciousness because they are born twice; once into the egg and once out of the egg. They are associated with rebirth and self-realization. Bird Woman is the Cancer goddess. She teaches us that, although we live in the illusion that security comes from our identity in the outer world, our true cosmic significance must be found within. Bird Woman directs us toward discovering our way home to our Soul, the place of lotus light. She has the ability to fly between Heaven and Earth, bringing communications from the angels and the spirit guides. She inspires souls to infuse matter with light – the true essence of co-creating.

Cancer Co-Creation Ideas

Now is the time to focus on...

- Being a good mother
- New ways to be a mom
- Nurturing and self-love
- The ability to see joy
- A clutter-free home
- My dream home
- Inner and outer security

On Your Altar

Colors: Shades of gray, milky/creamy colors

Numerology: 9 – let meditation nurture you

Tarot Card: Chariot – the ability to move forward, victory through action

Gemstones: Pearl, moonstone, ruby

Plant Remedy: Shooting Star – the ability to move straight ahead

Fragrance: Peppermint – the essence of the Great Mother

New Moon in Cancer

July 8, 12:15 AM

Cancer Challenges and Victories

Today I take advantage of my ability to take action and position myself for success. I clearly know that the road to success is before me, and all I need to do is move forward. I am aware that when I take action and move forward, the Universe fills in the dots. Whether I move left or right, or straight ahead doesn't matter—what matters is movement. Today, I release indecisiveness that keeps me stuck. Today, I let go of vacillation that exhausts my mind. Today, I take my foot off of the brakes and find the gas pedal. I allow movement to occur, even if I don't know where I am going. When I take action, I trust the guideposts will appear. I am aware that action leads me to my new direction. So, today I know and GO! I remember that Karma comes to the space of non-action, while success comes through action. Action brings me to my victory. Standing still leads to regret, resentment, and chaos. I am aware that action can be as simple as taking a walk on the beach, buying fresh flowers to add a new dimension to my home, or simply going to a new restaurant for lunch. I take action today to break up a crystallized pattern and, in so doing, my life begins to show me newfound awareness and light to guide me.

Cancer Homework

Cancer co-creates best when catering, writing cookbooks, marriage and family counseling, providing childcare, giving massage, or when engaged in genealogy, arts and crafts, architecture, and home building.

During the Cancer New Moon cycle, we are asked to create light into form and turn it into beauty on four levels. Physically, we must feel nurtured and protected. Emotionally, we must set safe boundaries for the expression of our feelings. Mentally, we must release self-pity and embrace rightful thinking. Spiritually, we must hold the space for the infusion of light to shine inside all bodies on Earth.

New Moon in Cancer

July 8, 12:15 AM

Five Steps to Co-Creation

1. Acceptance

Acceptance opens the pathway to living in the moment and makes way for opportunity to occur. Co-creation can only occur when you live in the moment.

Start your list by writing... "I accept _____ into my life."

2. Adjustment

Consider what adjustments you may need to make in order to receive what you are accepting into your life.

My Co-Creation List

new Moon in Cancer

July 8, 12:15 AM

3. Awakening

Once your list is complete, use the power of sound and read your list out loud. This directs your intentions (your list) toward actualization and co-creation.

4. Alignment

Now it is time to make a petition to the Universe, using these words, "I call on the power of the Universe to know I am ready to receive my list. I accept it. I allow it. So be it! This, or something better than this, comes to me in an easy and pleasurable way for the good of all concerned. Thank You Universe!" Light your candle and place it on your eight-sided mirror.

5. Acknowledgement

When a creation result is acknowledged it seals the deal. This makes room for more magnificence to expand into your life and increases your abundance factor adding to your ability to receive.

As each aspect of your co-creation list arrives in your life, spend time allowing, acknowledging, and accepting it with the true gusto of gratitude. You might want to make a victory list here.

Victory List

Cancer Questions to ask Myself

How can I nurture myself in a way that fills my heart?

What is the best way for me to heal my need for security?

How can I learn to share my feeling without complaining?

new Moon in Cancer

July 8, 12:15 AM

How to Use the Moon Book With Your Chart

Fill in the blanks on the Cosmic Check-In page. Then look up the degree of the moon on the chart below. Take note of the "I" statement on the outside of the wheel where the moon is located. Now locate the same degree on your own chart, and make a note of the house and corresponding "I" statement. Go back to the Cosmic Check-In page and circle the two statements from the charts and read what you wrote. This will give you an idea about what to expect from this moon phase on a personal level.

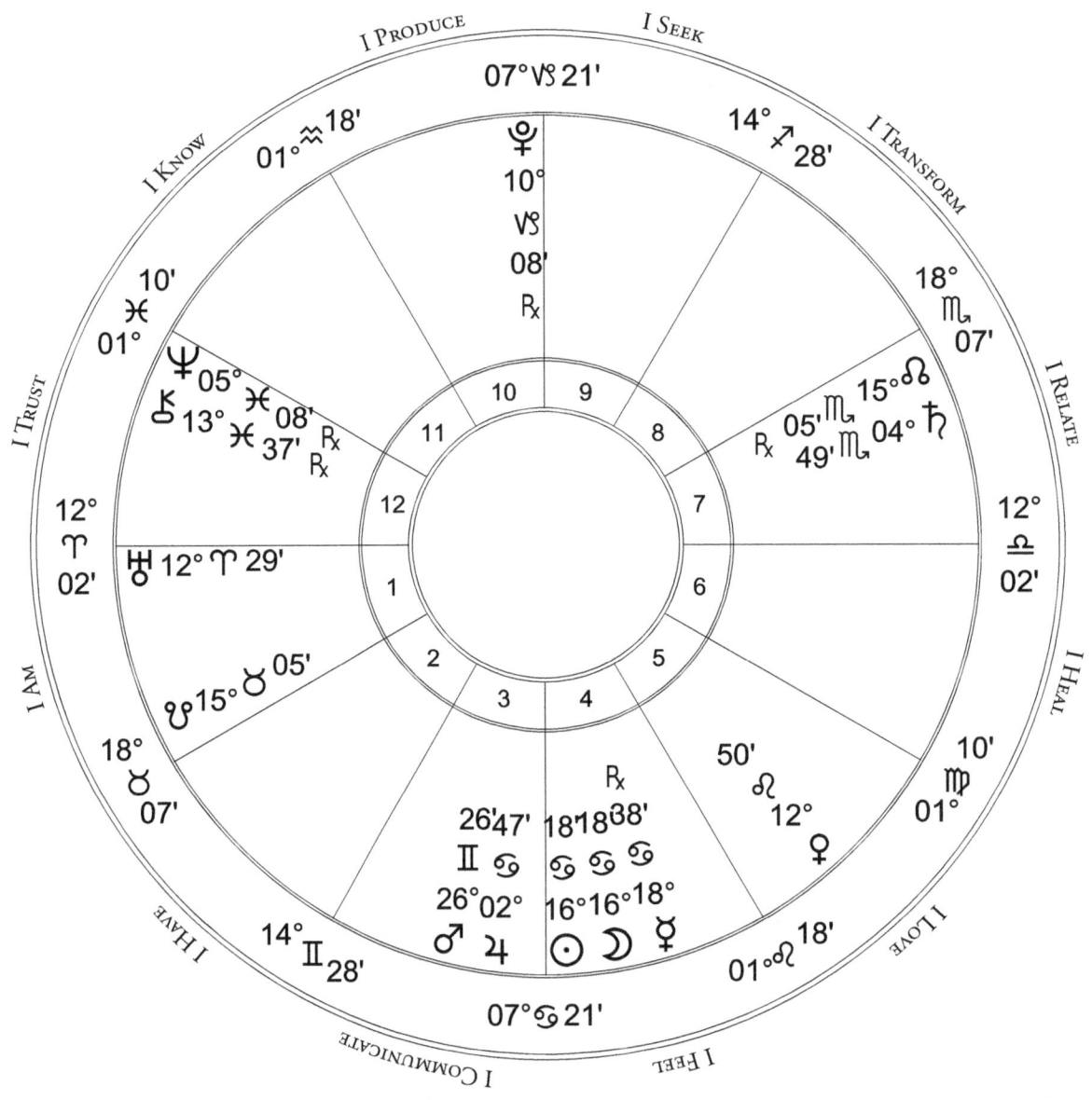

new Moon in Cancer

July 8, 12:15 AM

Cosmic Check-In

Take a moment to write a brief phrase for each "I" statement.
This activates all areas of your life for this creative cycle.

♋ I Feel

♌ I Love

♍ I Heal

♎ I Relate

♏ I Transform

♐ I Seek

♑ I Produce

♒ I Know

♓ I Trust

♈ I Am

♉ I Have

♊ I Communicate

Full Moon in Aquarius

July 22, 11:17 AM

Statement I Know
Body Ankles
Mind Abandonment Issues
Spirit Vision

The Sun is Opposite the Moon

Full Moons are always in opposition to the Sun. This creates a feeling of tension between where you want to shine and how your feelings are flowing on a sensory level about the Sun's directive. The two forces seem like they are working against each other, yet they are on the same team displaying different techniques to attain the same mission. The Aquarius/Leo polarity creates tension between the quest for group interaction and the recognition of self.

Aquarius Goddess

Hera, the Queen of Heaven, was responsible for every aspect of existence. Her name means "Great Lady." Legend has it that she created the Milky Way from the milk in her breasts. When the drops of milk came to Earth, white lily fields manifested everywhere. Hera was the only goddess who accompanied women through every aspect of their lives. She was the great protector of their marriages, their children, and their welfare. She was an advocate for women until she married Zeus and experienced a complete personality change, cursing all women in whom Zeus was interested sexually. Scorned, she turned vindictive toward the women who were the objects of Zeus' desire, rather that placing her rage on Zeus, where it belonged. Her jealously became her trademark. When the Moon is full in Aquarius we must learn the Art of Detachment so we don't sell out to emotional entrapments.

Aquarius Freedom List Ideas

Now is the time to free myself from…

- Resistance to authority figures
- Blocks to living in the moment
- Unnecessary rebellion
- Non-productive frenzy and fantasy
- Lack of spontaneity
- People who aren't team players

On Your Altar

Colors: Electric colors, neon, multi-colors

Numerology: 5 – promote action in your community

Tarot card: Star – being guided by a higher source

Gemstones: Aquamarine, amethyst, opal

Plant Remedy: Queen of the Night Cactus – the ability to see in the dark

Fragrance: Myrrh – healing the nervous system

Full Moon in Aquarius

July 22, 11:17 AM

Memory Maintenance Meditation

The Moon governs our memory and the maintenance of our memory. It is our memory that often creates blocks to setting us free to be able to attain our goals. The Moon works with us to help us become free from memory blocks three days after the Full Moon. The freedom themes are provided by the zodiac sign and can be from this lifetime or other lifetimes. These meditations assist in dissolving blocks and open pathways to new frontiers.

The Aquarius Full Moon promotes the rearrangement of plans. Find a way to quiet yourself. Sit down, close your eyes, and breathe in and out watching for a sudden change in priorities and an urge to express yourself more freely. Watch out for hyperactivity and carelessness. An unexpected breakthrough in an ungratifying situation can occur, sparking the creation of a new pathway. Take time to connect to angelic forces to see the other side of frenzy and fantasy, in order to know practical passion. Reconcile with times when your zeal has hurt others. Make contact with the magnetic energy currents of the atmosphere to recharge the body and behold the cosmic braille points of things to come. Receive instructions from the higher worlds to be the guardian of unknown, inventive treasures.

Aquarian Challenges and Victories

Today I let go. I trust that whatever breaks down or breaks through is a blessing in disguise for me. I make a commitment to allow myself to be spontaneous and live in the moment. I know the unexpected is a blessing for me and a way for me to make a break from my limitations. I am aware that I am resistant to change. I know I must make changes and I am too stubborn to take the appropriate action myself to change. I have built many walls of false protection around me, guarding me and blocking me from the reality that change is a constant. I have freeze-framed my life and desire support to update myself. I have allowed my fear of change to be my false motto and my life is at a standstill.

I am unwilling use any more energy to perpetuate my resistance. I know that continuing to cling to the past is a waste of my energy. I can no longer put things off that delay my process. I feel the breaking down of form. I trust that all changes are in my favor. All changes lead me to golden opportunities. I release false pride. I release false foundations. I release false authorities. In so doing, I allow for everything to crumble around me, so I can see that my true strength is within and I will build my life from the inside out. I am ready for new experiences. I am ready for the unexpected. I am willing to have an event occur, so that I can become activated towards my breakthrough. I am ready for the power of now. I know being spontaneous will bring me to true joy. I know if I ride this carrier wave it will take me to a place far beyond my scope of limited thinking. I know the will of God works in my favor and trust that it knows more than I do in any given moment.

Aquarian Homework

Go find yourself a soap box and use a natural setting as your audience. Voice all that you know to be true to the point of self-realization, where your authentic purpose can be revealed to you. This is the moment where you have released all that has kept you from your true sense of freedom. Remember to replenish all of the electrolytes in your system.

The Aquarius Full Moon reminds us of our connection to solar fire, the heart of the Sun, also known as the Heart of the Cosmos. During this time our vitality is recharged and our potent power comes into play, motivating the masses to receive more energy to transmute into the world.

Full Moon in Aquarius

July 22, 11:17 AM

Five Steps to Freedom

When we work with the concept of freedom we are soon presented with resistance. Freedom presents a pathway for us to bump directly into our limitations. When we can become aware of these limits, we can then find our way to freedom. Below are some ideas that might assist you in seeing deeper into your resistance to accepting freedom into your life. Once you discover these you might want to add more to your freedom list.

1. Feeling Useless

This happens when you measure yourself by what others think of you.

2. Discouragement

This occurs when you use blame others instead of taking responsibility for your part in a situation.

3. Regret

This happens when you live inside past events and continue to rehearse your story, hoping that if you tell it enough, it will get resolved. Living in the past leads to regret and blocks you from freedom.

4. Limitation

This happens when we think that there is no way out of a challenge, which creates an inability to see options. When options are out of the picture we become unable to create positive outcomes.

5. Self-Doubt

This takes place when we think that others are better than we are. Growing cannot occur when we have given someone else our ceiling.

Full Moon in Aquarius

July 22, 11:17 AM

My Freedom List

Aquarian Questions to Ask Myself

Where do I still think inside the box?

How willing am I to be spontaneous without rebellion?

Am I contributing to my team in a way that makes the future better?

Where is my elitism playing out and leaving me out of the fun?

full Moon in Aquarius

July 22, 11:17 AM

How to Use the Moon Book With Your Chart

Fill in the blanks on the Cosmic Check-In page. Then look up the degree of the moon on the chart below. Take note of the "I" statement on the outside of the wheel where the moon is located. Now locate the same degree on your own chart, and make a note of the house and corresponding "I" statement. Go back to the Cosmic Check-In page and circle the two statements from the charts and read what you wrote. This will give you an idea about what to expect from this moon phase on a personal level.

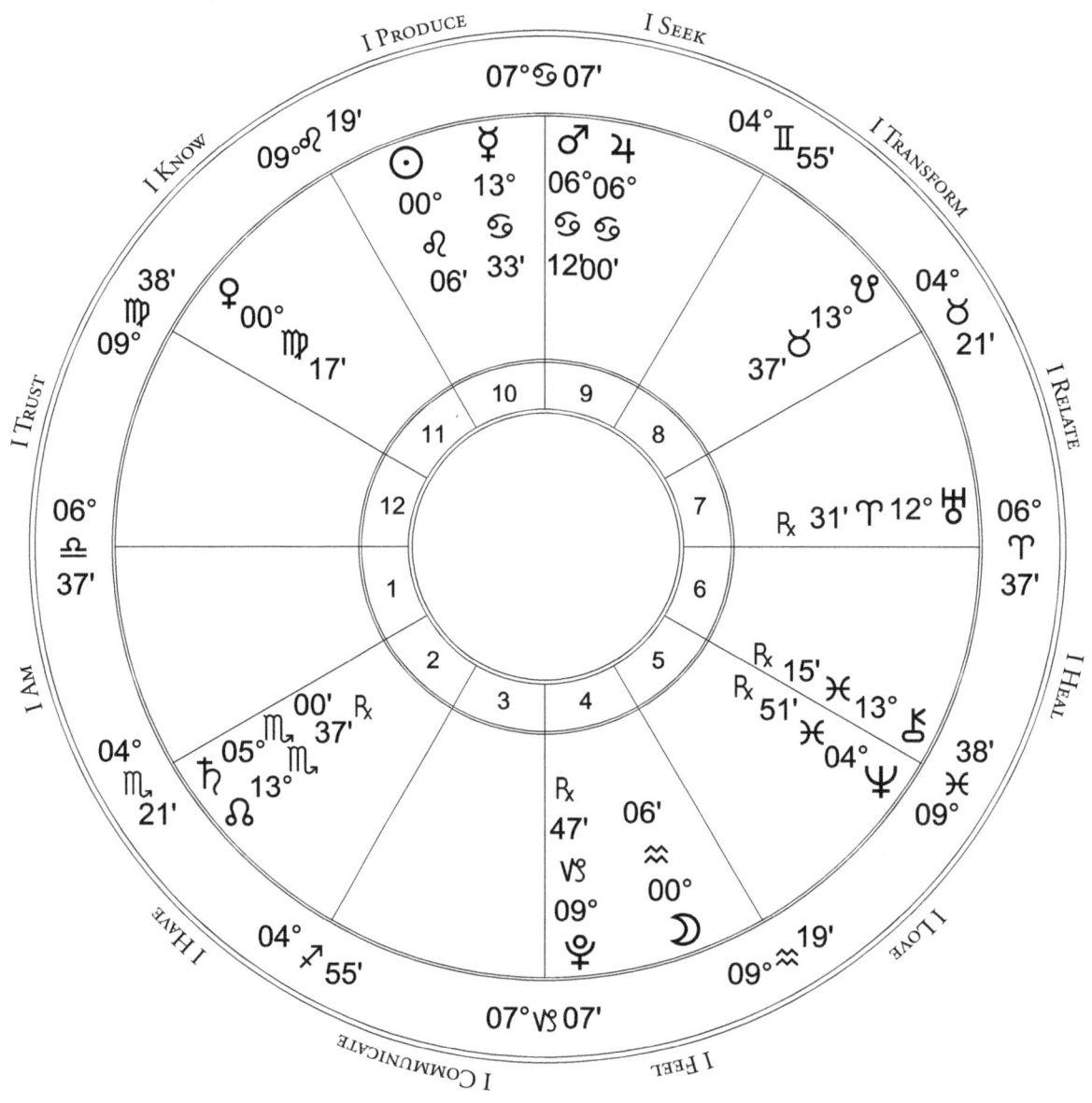

♈ Aries	♋ Cancer	♏ Scorpio	♓ Pisces	♀ Venus	♅ Uranus	☊ North Node
♉ Taurus	♌ Leo	♐ Sagittarius	☉ Sun	♂ Mars	♆ Neptune	☋ South Node
♊ Gemini	♍ Virgo	♑ Capricorn	☽ Moon	♃ Jupiter	♀ or ♇ Pluto	℞ Retrograde
	♎ Libra	♒ Aquarius	☿ Mercury	♄ Saturn	⚷ Chiron	

full Moon in Aquarius

July 22, 11:17 AM

Cosmic Check-In

Take a moment to write a brief phrase for each "I" statement.
This activates all areas of your life for this freedom cycle.

♒ I Know

♓ I Trust

♈ I Am

♉ I Have

♊ I Communicate

♋ I Feel

♌ I Love

♍ I Heal

♎ I Relate

♏ I Transform

♐ I Seek

♑ I Produce

August 2013

SUN	MON	TUE	WED	THU	FRI	SAT
				1 ♇♆♅⚷℞▼ ☽ V/C 9:49 AM 6. Be willing to forgive.	**2** ♇♆♅⚷℞▼ ☽ → ♋ 9:30 PM 7. Create peacefulness in your mind.	**3** ♇♆♅⚷℞ 8. Be open to new avenues of income.
4 ♇♆♅⚷℞ ☽ V/C 11:50 PM 9. Be at peace with all around you.	**5** ♇♆♅⚷℞ ☽ → ♌ 9:59 AM 10. You are capable in all situations.	**6** ♇♆♅⚷℞ ● 14°♌35′ 2:52 PM ☽ V/C 2:52 PM 2. Choose balance and harmony in life.	**7** ♇♆♅⚷℞ ☽ → ♍ 8:58 PM 3. Go to a happy, funny movie.	**8** ♇♆♅⚷℞ ☿ → ♌ 5:14 AM 5. You can change your thinking.	**9** ♇♆♅⚷℞ ☽ V/C 3:06 PM 6. Know that you are loving and loveable.	**10** ♇♆♅⚷℞ ☽ → ♎ 6:09 AM 7. Release all fears and doubts.
11 ♇♆♅⚷℞ ☽ V/C 6:30 PM 8. Accept the best.	**12** ♇♆♅⚷℞ ☽ → ♏ 1:19 PM 9. See with compassion and understanding.	**13** ♇♆♅⚷℞ 10. Every thought creates your future.	**14** ♇♆♅⚷℞ ☽ V/C 2:31 PM ☽ → ♐ 6:05 PM 2. Balance your male and female polarities.	**15** ♇♆♅⚷℞▲ 3. Make life simple and easy.	**16** ♇♆♅⚷℞▲ ♀ → ♎ 8:38 AM ☽ V/C 10:33 AM ☽ → ♑ 8:26 PM 4. Discover your authentic self.	**17** ♇♆♅⚷℞ 5. Be willing to make changes.
18 ♇♆♅⚷℞ ☽ V/C 11:27 AM ☽ → ♒ 9:08 PM 6. Have a mellow night at home.	**19** ♇♆♅⚷℞ 7. Self discovery is always safe.	**20** ♇♆♅⚷℞ ○ 28°♒11′ 6:46 PM ☽ V/C 6:46 PM ☽ → ♓ 9:44 PM 8. Prosper wherever you turn.	**21** ♇♆♅⚷℞ 9. Feel compassion and love for all.	**22** ♇♆♅⚷℞ ☉ → ♍ 4:03 PM ☽ V/C 6:39 PM 10. Freely move beyond limitations.	**23** ♇♆♅⚷℞ ☽ → ♈ 12:14 AM ☿ → ♍ 3:37 PM 2. Balance work and play.	**24** ♇♆♅⚷℞ 3. Use your unique and creative talents.
25 ♇♆♅⚷℞ ☽ V/C 3:03 AM ☽ → ♉ 6:14 AM 4. Be dependable, but not dependent.	**26** ♇♆♅⚷℞ 5. Add variety in your life.	**27** ♇♆♅⚷℞ ☽ V/C 3:59 PM ☽ → ♊ 4:09 PM ♂ → ♌ 7:06 PM 6. First help yourself and then others.	**28** ♇♆♅⚷℞ ☽ V/C 9:45 PM 7. Add a new word to your vocabulary.	**29** ♇♆♅⚷℞▼ 8. Be self-reliant.	**30** ♇♆♅⚷℞▼ ☽ → ♋ 4:34 AM 9. Live your divine birthright.	**31** ♇♆♅⚷℞ ☽ V/C 5:06 PM 10. Fresh new experiences are ahead.

August 2013 Planetary Highlights

Pluto Retrograde in Capricorn all Month

Create a dream team of experts to work with and feel the support of prosperity that comes when a team is in place. Remember that the Earth is abundant and there will always be an exchange rate.

Neptune Retrograde in Pisces all Month

Take time out in your personal studies to learn the difference between conditional love and unconditional love. Remember that love is a principle, not a practice. It is not how you act or who you are with. Learn where you step out of love and check to see what soul state has you … is it grief, guilt, fear, or anger? Honor whatever shows up, work with it in the moment, and return to love.

Uranus Retrograde in Aries all Month

Proceed with caution and slow down. Keep higher awareness in your experience and know everything else is transitory. Finish old projects.

Chiron Retrograde in Pisces all Month

Keep a compassionate heart and share what you know to help those who are feeling confused right now. Remember that creativity heals.

August 7 – Uranus in Aries and Pluto in Capricorn

This creates tension between your need for security in the old world support structure that is decaying every moment and your new frontiers asking you to have enough trust to go beyond the known to the new frontiers.

August 8 – Pluto, Uranus, Mars and Jupiter

Tension could grow to a global level looking for battle fields to fight as the old guard takes on a deeper resistance to accept change.

August 8, 5:14 AM – Mercury enters Leo

The communicator enters the love zone and the possibilities for win-win solutions can manifest.

August 16, 8:38 AM – Venus enters Libra

It's a miracle—the language of the heart-mind moves into place and diplomacy becomes a standard for the next four weeks. Plus, there will be a bit of drama in true Leo style.

August 22, 4:03 PM – The Sun enters Virgo

The energy moves from the highest point of light to the tiny details relating to work, health, and healing.

August 23, 3:37 PM – Mercury enters Virgo

Mercury loves Virgo! Use this to your advantage and clean out your office or your body.

August 25 – A Grand Cross between Venus, Jupiter, Pluto, and Uranus

This opens a pathway to abundance on the world front. Keep your abundance basket open and let the gold pour in to your life.

August 26 – Neptune and the Sun Oppose Each Other

This brings a choice between denial and deception or compassion and idealism. It is a good idea to use oppositions for integration rather than separation. Pick two of these points and see if you can marry them. Expect to be a bit foggy or dizzy on this day.

August 27, 7:06 PM – Mars enters Leo

We are in double fire for the next six weeks. Fire meets passion during this time. Make love not war! Tons of energy to move mountains. Avoid burn out!

August 15 and 16 – Super-Sensitivity ▲

Do your best to stay out of the chaotic vortex in the atmosphere. Loss of focus could be harmful and possibly depressing. Stay close to home if you can.

August 1 and 2, 29 and 30 – Low-Vitality ▼

Earth changes are possible on these days. Be Prepared. Take time out and go with the flow. Get rest!

♈ Aries	♋ Cancer	♐ Sagittarius	☽ Moon	♄ Saturn	☊ North Node	V/C Void-of-Course
♉ Taurus	♌ Leo	♑ Capricorn	☿ Mercury	♅ Uranus	☋ South Node	▲ Super-Sensitivity
♊ Gemini	♍ Virgo	♒ Aquarius	♀ Venus	♆ Neptune	➡ Enters	▼ Low-Vitality
	♎ Libra	♓ Picses	♂ Mars	♀ or ♇ Pluto	℞ Retrograde	
	♏ Scorpio	☉ Sun	♃ Jupiter	⚷ Chiron	S/D Stationary Direct	

New Moon in Leo

August 6, 2:52 PM

Statement   I Love
Body   Heart
Mind   Creativity
Spirit   Good use of will

When the Sun is in Leo

This is the time when we feel the power from the Sun, the heart of the Cosmos. Leo has a direct relationship with the Sun's heart. The Sun rules your identity. Now is the time to shine and stand tall in the center of your life. Allow yourself to feel the power of your individual conscious Self. When we align with the power of the Sun, we become radiant. This radiance gives us the power to transmit energy into life. Personal fulfillment becomes a reality when we align our will with love. Remember to live love every day!

Leo Goddess

The sun goddess makes her appearance when the Sun is setting. She paints with the vast pallet of colors available as the day turns to night. She infuses tomorrow's dreams and goals with vitality. She lives in the West where the feminine principle lives. She teaches us to express our creative power potential. She reminds us that the promise of tomorrow comes when we live in truth and integrity and follow the light of our awareness, even through the dark. When the flash of green appears to us at sunset, we know we have connected with the sun goddess.

Leo Co-Creation Ideas

Now is the time to focus on…

- New love or new ways of loving
- New creative ways of expressing myself
- Bonding with those I love
- Quality time with those I love
- Knowledge of my soul's intention
- Fun with my children
- Being a bright beaming light
- Connecting to the hearts of humanity

On Your Altar

Colors: Royal purple, royal blue, orange

Numerology: 2 – live in harmony

Tarot Card: Sun – to stand tall in the center of life

Gemstones: Peridot, emerald, amber

Plant Remedy: Sunflower – standing tall in the center of your garden

Fragrance: Jasmine – remembering your Soul's original intention

new Moon in Leo

August 6, 2:52 PM

Leo Challenges and Victories

Today I am at the center of bliss, happiness, abundance, and total celebration. It is my time to shine and feel the power of my true self blasting the Universe, the entire planet, and all of life with the light of my awareness. There is nothing that can stop me today, because I am free to be me. When I am free to be me, I can stand naked in the daylight and have nothing to hide. I truly know that all of life loves me and I love all of life. I feel the radiance and vibration of my being activating me with aliveness, vitality, and charisma. I know that I can make a difference because I celebrate life by infusing, sparking, and igniting matter with light. I am open and ready to embrace all that comes to me with joy. I say "yes!" to all opportunities today; knowing that today is my day. I am in the flow of abundance and I let abundance flow through me.

The child within me is open and ready to play full out; there is not a cloud in the sky today that can eclipse me or place a shadow on me and keep me from my true level of power. I am aware that the child state of being within me simply says yes to action and action is power. When I take action today, my possibilities are endless because they are generated from my true self and motivated by happiness, joy, and freedom. The child within me is able to play full out because I have birthed myself beyond my old perception of blocks. I know that in taking this true power, to be motivated by happiness, pathways on all levels and in all dimensions can open to the empowerment of joy. Empowerment is mine today because I am shining from within myself and I know my deepest self is connected to the source. Empowerment occurs when I live from the inside out. Today, I wave the banner of my being from within, feel the glow, and go.

Leo Homework

The Leo co-creates best through fashion and jewelry design, glamour, politics, super-modeling, movie stardom, child advocacy, fundraising, toy and game design, image consulting, authoring children's books, sales, and cardiology.

Leo gets us closer to our essential self, reminding us of our Soul's original intention. We become ready to receive the benefits of reflective light and radiating light at the same time so that we can see our personality and our soul connecting to love which constitutes a new level of fulfillment. Expect purification, transmutation, communication, and mastery to be part of your personal experience.

New Moon in Leo

August 6, 2:52 PM

Five Steps to Co-Creation

1. Acceptance

Acceptance opens the pathway to living in the moment and makes way for opportunity to occur. Co-creation can only occur when you live in the moment.

Start your list by writing… "I accept _____ into my life."

2. Adjustment

Consider what adjustments you may need to make in order to receive what you are accepting into your life.

My Co-Creation List

new Moon in Leo

August 6, 2:52 PM

3. Awakening

Once your list is complete, use the power of sound and read your list out loud. This directs your intentions (your list) toward actualization and co-creation.

4. Alignment

Now it is time to make a petition to the Universe, using these words, "I call on the power of the Universe to know I am ready to receive my list. I accept it. I allow it. So be it! This, or something better than this, comes to me in an easy and pleasurable way for the good of all concerned. Thank You Universe!" Light your candle and place it on your eight-sided mirror.

5. Acknowledgement

When a creation result is acknowledged it seals the deal. This makes room for more magnificence to expand into your life and increases your abundance factor adding to your ability to receive.

As each aspect of your co-creation list arrives in your life, spend time allowing, acknowledging, and accepting it with the true gusto of gratitude. You might want to make a victory list here.

Victory List

Leo Questions to ask Myself

How can I reconstruct myself so I can grow into my true potential?

What can I do to get to a place of unconditional confidence?

How can I re-align my soul when everything is changing in the outside world?

new Moon in Leo

August 6, 2:52 PM

How to Use the Moon Book With Your Chart

Fill in the blanks on the Cosmic Check-In page. Then look up the degree of the moon on the chart below. Take note of the "I" statement on the outside of the wheel where the moon is located. Now locate the same degree on your own chart, and make a note of the house and corresponding "I" statement. Go back to the Cosmic Check-In page and circle the two statements from the charts and read what you wrote. This will give you an idea about what to expect from this moon phase on a personal level.

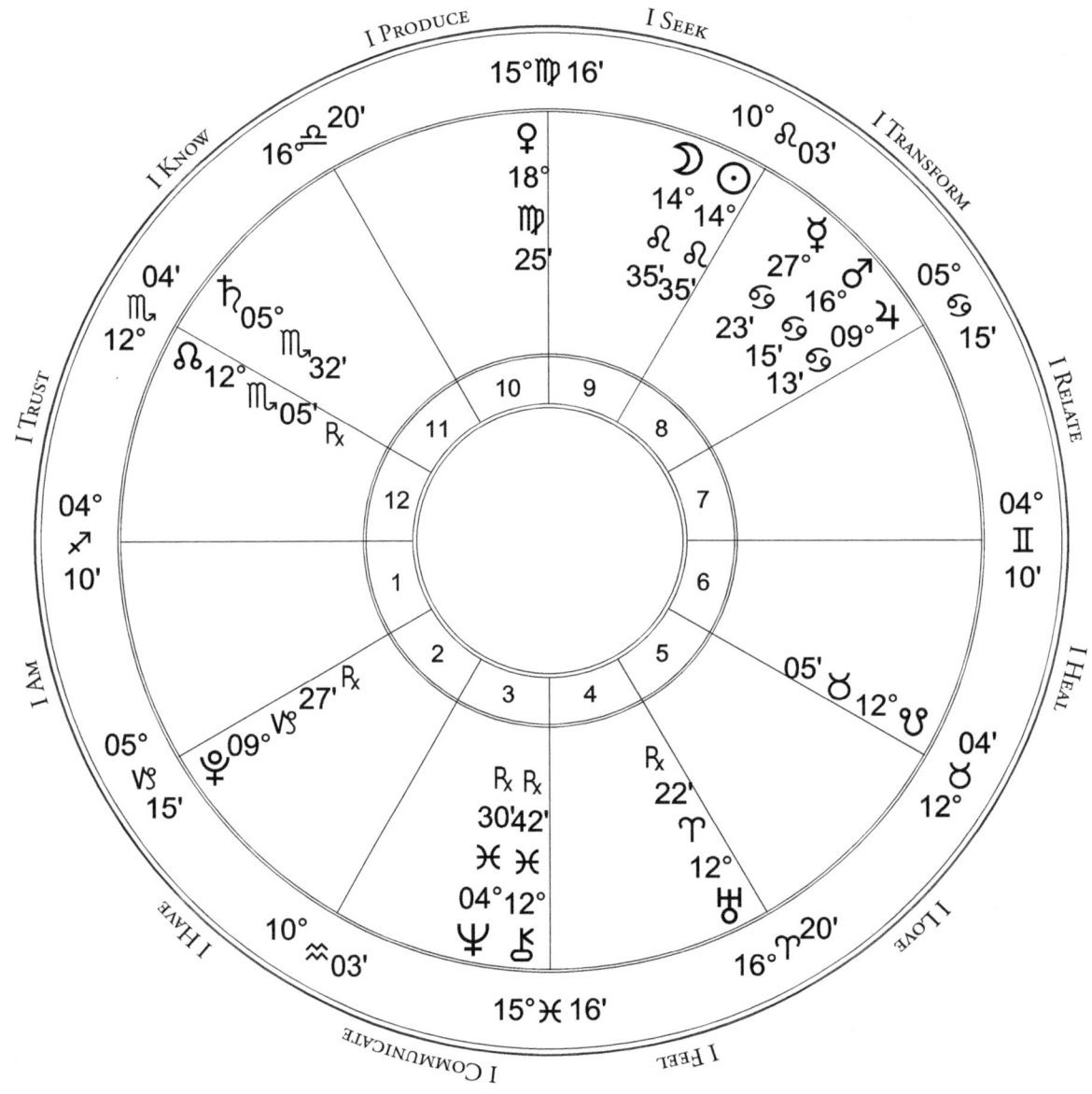

♈ Aries	♋ Cancer	♏ Scorpio	♓ Pisces	♀ Venus	♅ Uranus	☊ North Node
♉ Taurus	♌ Leo	♐ Sagittarius	☉ Sun	♂ Mars	♆ Neptune	☋ South Node
♊ Gemini	♍ Virgo	♑ Capricorn	☽ Moon	♃ Jupiter	♀ or ♇ Pluto	℞ Retrograde
	♎ Libra	♒ Aquarius	☿ Mercury	♄ Saturn	⚷ Chiron	

144

New Moon in Leo

August 6, 2:52 PM

Cosmic Check-In

Take a moment to write a brief phrase for each "I" statement.
This activates all areas of your life for this creative cycle.

♌ I Love

♍ I Heal

♎ I Relate

♏ I Transform

♐ I Seek

♑ I Produce

♒ I Know

♓ I Trust

♈ I Am

♉ I Have

♊ I Communicate

♋ I Feel

Full Moon in Aquarius

August 20, 6:46 PM

Statement I Know
Body Ankles
Mind Abandonment issues
Spirit Vision

The Sun is Opposite the Moon

Full Moons are always in opposition to the Sun. This creates a feeling of tension between where you want to shine and how your feelings are flowing on a sensory level about the Sun's directive. The two forces seem like they are working against each other, yet they are on the same team displaying different techniques to attain the same mission. The Aquarius/Leo polarity creates tension between the quest for group interaction and recognition of self.

Aquarius Goddess

Hera, the Queen of Heaven, was responsible for every aspect of existence. Her name means "Great Lady." Legend has it that she created the Milky Way from the milk in her breasts. When the drops of milk came to Earth, white lily fields manifested everywhere. Hera was the only goddess who accompanied women through every aspect of their lives. She was the great protector of their marriages, their children, and their welfare. She was an advocate for women until she married Zeus and had a complete personality change, cursing all women in whom Zeus was interested sexually. Scorned, she turned vindictive toward the women who were the objects of Zeus' desire, rather that placing her rage on Zeus, where it belonged. Her jealously became her trademark. When the Moon is full in Aquarius we must learn the Art of Detachment so we don't sell out to emotional entrapments.

Aquarius Freedom List Ideas

Now is the time to free myself from…

- Resistance to authority figures
- Blocks to living in the moment
- Unnecessary rebellion
- Non-productive frenzy and fantasy
- The need to be spontaneous
- People who aren't team players

On Your Altar

Colors: Electric colors, neon, multi-colors, pearl white

Numerology: 5 – Promote action in your community.

Tarot card: Star – being guided by a higher source

Gemstones: Aquamarine, amethyst, opal

Plant Remedy: Queen of the Night Cactus – the ability to see in the dark

Fragrance: Myrrh – healing the nervous system

Full Moon in Aquarius

August 20, 6:46 PM

Memory Maintenance Meditation

The Moon governs our memory and the maintenance of our memory. It is our memory that often creates blocks to setting us free to be able to attain our goals. The Moon works with us to help us become free from memory blocks three days after the Full Moon. The freedom themes are provided by the zodiac sign and can be from this lifetime or other lifetimes. These meditations assist in dissolving blocks and open pathways to new frontiers.

The Aquarius Full Moon promotes the rearrangement of plans. Sit quietly and close your eyes, breathe in and breathe out while watching for sudden changes in priorities and an urge to express yourself more freely. Watch out for hyperactivity and carelessness. The unexpected breakthrough in an ungratifying situation can occur, sparking the creation of a new pathway. Take time to connect to angelic forces to see the other side of frenzy and fantasy in order to know practical passion. Reconcile with times when your zeal has hurt others. Make contact with the magnetic energy currents of the atmosphere to recharge the body and behold the cosmic braille points of things to come. Receive instructions from the higher worlds to be the guardian of the unknown inventive treasures.

Aquarian Challenges and Victories

Today my true potential can be realized. All I have to do is take a risk and know that my faith is in operation. My future is very bright and offers me a promise of things to come. Today is a day of destiny. I have chosen this day to determine a DESTINY PROMISE I MADE TO MYSELF BEFORE I CAME INTO THIS LIFE. All that is required of me is to move out of my comfort zone and take a risk. I am aware that faith cannot be determined without risk, and I will take the risk to move into the next space of creation in my life. I release fear and move into faith, knowing full well that my logic and reason are part of the fear that keeps me stuck.

I am reminded that the kingdom of heaven is open to the child. I find the child within me today to embrace what life has for me with open arms and a spirit of adventure. I know my true potential lives inside my magical child and she/he is willing to play and go for the gusto. I am here in this life to fulfill my promise to experience life to the fullest and to release the fear of judgment that has hounded me and kept me from playing full-out. I remember that when I experience, I gather a knowledge base within my Soul and keep my agreement with myself and the Universe. I connect to my super-consciousness and take on the bigger view of my life and all that it has to offer me when I risk reason and take a leap of faith. I know in the depth of my awareness that, if I jump off the diving board, there will be water in the pool. I am willing to risk reason for an experience. Everything I ever wanted is one step outside my comfort zone. I go for the GUSTO today! I release my fear today and turn it into faith. I trust in the promise of things to come. I know my potential is realized today, and that all I have to do is say "yes!" to life!

Aquarian Homework

The Aquarius moon reminds us of our connection to solar fire (the heart of the Sun) also known as the Heart of the Cosmos. During this time, we get our vitality recharged and our potent power comes into play motivating the masses to receive more energy to transmute into the new world. Voice all that you know to be true to the point of self-realization where your authentic purpose can be revealed to you. This is the moment where you have released all that has kept you from your true sense of freedom. Remember to replenish all the electrolytes in your system.

Full Moon in Aquarius

August 20, 6:46 PM

Five Steps to Freedom

When we work with the concept of freedom we are soon presented with resistance. Freedom presents a pathway for us to bump directly into our limitations. When we can become aware of these limits, we can then find our way to freedom. Below are some ideas that might assist you in seeing deeper into your resistance to accepting freedom into your life. Once you discover these you might want to add more to your freedom list.

1. Feeling Useless

This happens when you measure yourself by what others think of you.

2. Discouragement

This occurs when you use blame others instead of taking responsibility for your part in a situation.

3. Regret

This happens when you live inside past events and continue to rehearse your story, hoping that if you tell it enough, it will get resolved. Living in the past leads to regret and blocks you from freedom.

4. Limitation

This happens when we think that there is no way out of a challenge, which creates an inability to see options. When options are out of the picture we become unable to create positive outcomes.

5. Self-Doubt

This takes place when we think that others are better than we are. Growing cannot occur when we have given someone else our ceiling.

Full Moon in Aquarius

August 20, 6:46 PM

My Freedom List

Aquarian Questions to Ask Myself

How can I contribute to the new myth of creation on Earth?

Am I ready to accept the many changes and challenges required on the behalf of ascension; being completely rearranged while living a life designed to get everyone where they need to be?

How can I harmonize with the new mysteries and express myself as a part of the awakening team?

Full Moon in Aquarius

August 20, 6:46 PM

How to Use the Moon Book With Your Chart

Fill in the blanks on the Cosmic Check-In page. Then look up the degree of the moon on the chart below. Take note of the "I" statement on the outside of the wheel where the moon is located. Now locate the same degree on your own chart, and make a note of the house and corresponding "I" statement. Go back to the Cosmic Check-In page and circle the two statements from the charts and read what you wrote. This will give you an idea about what to expect from this moon phase on a personal level.

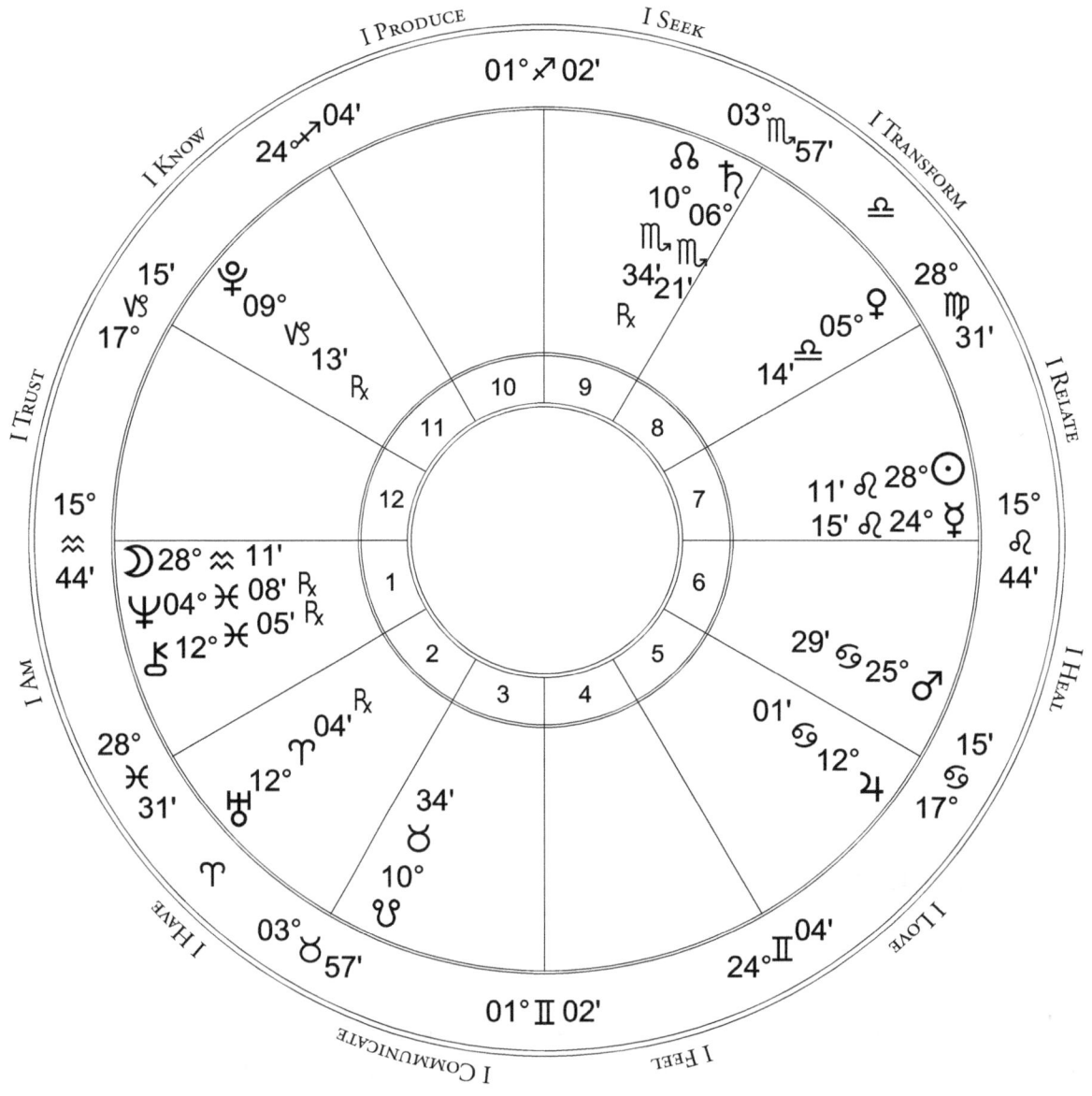

♈ Aries	♋ Cancer	♏ Scorpio	♓ Pisces	♀ Venus	♅ Uranus	☊ North Node
♉ Taurus	♌ Leo	♐ Sagittarius	☉ Sun	♂ Mars	♆ Neptune	☋ South Node
♊ Gemini	♍ Virgo	♑ Capricorn	☽ Moon	♃ Jupiter	♀ or ♇ Pluto	℞ Retrograde
	♎ Libra	♒ Aquarius	☿ Mercury	♄ Saturn	⚷ Chiron	

full Moon in Aquarius

August 20, 6:46 PM

Cosmic Check-In

Take a moment to write a brief phrase for each "I" statement.
This activates all areas of your life for this freedom cycle.

♒ I Know

♓ I Trust

♈ I Am

♉ I Have

♊ I Communicate

♋ I Feel

♌ I Love

♍ I Heal

♎ I Relate

♏ I Transform

♐ I Seek

♑ I Produce

September 2013

SUN	MON	TUE	WED	THU	FRI	SAT
1 ♇♆♅⚷℞ ☽ → ♌ 5:02 PM 2. Do not go to extremes.	**2** ♇♆♅⚷℞ Labor Day 3. Embrace your unique creative talents.	**3** ♇♆♅⚷℞ ☽ V/C 10:53 AM 4. A sense of order works.	**4** ♇♆♅⚷℞ Rosh Hashanah ☽ → ♍ 3:44 AM 5. Flow with the cycles of change.	**5** ♇♆♅⚷℞ ● 13°♍04' 4:37 AM 6. Wherever you are right now is perfect.	**6** ♇♆♅⚷℞ ☽ V/C 3:11 AM ☽ → ♎ 12:13 PM 7. Trust your inner wisdom.	**7** ♇♆♅⚷℞ 8. Be fulfilled in all that you do.
8 ♇♆♅⚷℞ ☽ V/C 1:47 PM ☽ → ♏ 6:45 PM 9. Your intuition is always on your side.	**9** ♇♆♅⚷℞ ☿ → ♎ 12:08 AM 10. Each day is totally new. Enjoy!	**10** ♇♆♅⚷℞ ☽ V/C 2:22 AM ♀ → ♏ 11:17 PM ☽ → ♐ 11:37 PM 2. Gather opinions and then decide.	**11** ♇♆♅⚷℞ 3. A worrisome attitude wastes energy.	**12** ♇♆♅⚷℞▲ ☽ V/C 10:09 AM 4. Approach life sensibly and find joy.	**13** ♇♆♅⚷℞▲ Yom Kippur ☽ → ♑ 2:57 AM 5. Intend and be willing to change.	**14** ♇♆♅⚷℞ ☽ V/C 4:18 PM 6. Handle any health issues immediately.
15 ♇♆♅⚷℞ ☽ → ♒ 5:06 AM 7. You will know what you need to know in the moment.	**16** ♇♆♅⚷℞ ☽ V/C 1:20 AM 8. Prosperity directs you at every turn.	**17** ♇♆♅⚷℞ ☽ → ♓ 6:59 AM 9. Create a sacred place in your home.	**18** ♇♆♅⚷℞ 10. Be open to new & glorious experiences.	**19** ♇♆♅⚷℞ ○ 26°♓41' 4:14 AM ☽ V/C 4:14 AM ☽ → ♈ 9:59 AM 2. Look at both sides of an issue.	**20** ♆♅⚷℞ ♇D-8°♑59' 8:28 AM ☽ V/C 6:26 PM 3. You are free to believe what you wish.	**21** ♆♅⚷℞ ☽ → ♉ 3:34 PM 4. Be a dependable friend.
22 ♆♅⚷℞ Fall Equinox ☉ → ♎ 1:45 PM 5. Choose to respond instead of reacting.	**23** ♆♅⚷℞ ☽ V/C 12:14 AM 6. Does your environment reflect you?	**24** ♆♅⚷℞ ☽ → ♊ 12:35 AM 7. Focus on what makes you happy.	**25** ♆♅⚷℞▼ 8. Accept only the best in life.	**26** ♆♅⚷℞▼ ☽ V/C 4:22 AM ☽ → ♋ 12:25 PM 9. Envision Universal peace and harmony.	**27** ♆♅⚷℞ 10. Greet the future with open arms.	**28** ♆♅⚷℞ 2. Intend to make the right choices.
29 ♆♅⚷℞ ☽ V/C 12:31 AM ☽ → ♌ 12:58 AM ☿ → ♏ 4:39 AM 3. Enjoy a laugh with a friend.	**30** ♆♅℞ ☽ V/C 9:49 PM 4. Work in a format that suits you.					

September 2013 Planetary Highlights

September 20, 8:28 AM – Pluto in Capricorn goes out of Retrograde

Check to see what you have re-translated regarding the systems or structures in your life. Give yourself credit if something has moved out of resistance and some space has become evident. Consider options to make positive outcomes occur.

Neptune in Pisces is Retrograde all Month

The best approach here is to sink yourself into a service program that makes you aware that there are bigger and better formulas for healing yourself, rather than suffering over what you perceive as a loss. Transmute empathy into compassion and all will go well.

Uranus in Aries is Retrograde all Month

Exploration toward new frontiers will seem slower right now. Uranus wants radical change and asks you to forget about what anyone else wants or thinks in order to apply these changes for yourself. Change of this magnitude needs the brakes applied to it at some point; if only to ensure that you don't fly off the road. Use this time to clarify your breakthrough limits and integrate what you have already changed. Place your attention and focus on anything you've missed or shied away from. If you are accepting the new directions, this energy will ensure that you're on the right track.

Chiron in Pisces is Retrograde all Month

Allow yourself to feel the water element teaching you to take the line of least resistance. Learn to flow with the water and let yourself heal.

September 9, 12:08 AM – Mercury Moves into Libra

Because of the duplicity of Mercury and the rationalizations of Libra's need to know about all sides to any equation, it is not a good idea to even try to make any decisions right now. Do what you can to stay in the center of life for the next three weeks.

September 10, 11:17 PM – Venus enters Scorpio

Scorpio loves silence and Venus loves to chat which brings about an interesting pattern of diversity. Venus wants to make love and Scorpio wants to have sex. If Venus doesn't get what she wants, she could engage in some games that would make Scorpio jealous. Do what you can to avoid this! The "ouch" could become a deep pain to be reckoned with at a later date. Intimacy is the answer here.

September 11-14 – Venus, Saturn and the North Node meet up in Scorpio

This creates a disheartening struggle between love, money, sex, and being accountable. The Scorpio storage bank of undelivered feelings can become unbearable if not directed carefully.

September 14 – Uranus and Mars join in the game to break up the Scorpion Resistance

Stay out of the way and let the changes happen. It could be a blessing or a curse depending on how you view the breakthrough. Go with the flow and hold on to your highest thought.

September 22, 1:45 PM – Fall Equinox – Sun Moves into Libra

It is harvest time. Do an inventory and ask yourself, "Did I meet my goals that I set for myself last Spring?"

September 29, 4:39 AM – Mercury enters Scorpio

Watch out for sarcasm when communicating. Scorpio stuffs its closet full of undelivered communications and now is the time to empty out the closet. The sting is in operation here—watch out!

September 12 and 13 – Super-Sensitivity ▲

The global atmosphere is very chaotic, stagnant, and toxic all at the same time. If you personalize it you could become depressed. Don't push. Go slow and stay close to home.

September 25 and 26 – Low-Vitality ▼

The Earth energy is in need of rejuvenation. Help her by taking good care of yourself on these days. Trust in the completion process and let things come to an end so that new paradigms can occur faster and bring new energy to us.

♈ Aries	♋ Cancer	♐ Sagittarius	☽ Moon	♄ Saturn	☊ North Node	V/C Void-of-Course
♉ Taurus	♌ Leo	♑ Capricorn	☿ Mercury	♅ Uranus	☋ South Node	▲ Super-Sensitivity
♊ Gemini	♍ Virgo	♒ Aquarius	♀ Venus	♆ Neptune	→ Enters	▼ Low-Vitality
	♎ Libra	♓ Pisces	♂ Mars	♀ or ♇ Pluto	℞ Retrograde	
	♏ Scorpio	☉ Sun	♃ Jupiter	⚷ Chiron	S/D Stationary Direct	

new Moon in Virgo

September 5, 4:37 AM

Statement I Heal
Body Intestines
Mind Critical
Spirit Divinity in the details

When the Sun is in Virgo

Virgo is called the "Womb of Time," in which the seeds of great value are planted, shielded, nourished, and revealed. It is the labor of Virgo that brings the Christ Principle into manifestation within individuals and mankind. This unification occurs when we feel the power within us to serve. When we serve, we give birth to Divinity. Virgo time is when we all have a chance to raise the standard of excellence in our lives and on the Earth. The Virgo intelligence stores and maintains light in a precise manner. Attention to detail is Virgo's great gift to life.

Virgo Goddess

The Virgo goddess, Cosmic Womb Woman, gives birth to Divinity. She is a symbol of the ability to give birth to the Self in order to serve, perfect, and purify. It is Cosmic Womb Woman who urges each human to fulfill the goal of evolution by planting seeds of love and power, sending the spark of light to each atom, plant, animal, and planet in the entire solar system.

Virgo Co-Creation Ideas

Now is the time to focus on...

- A high standard of excellence
- A healthy lifestyle
- Self-acceptance
- Discernment without judgment
- Healing abilities
- Contribution to Nature
- A healthy body

On Your Altar

Colors: Earth tones, blue, green

Numerology: 6 – Celebrate health, love, and beauty

Tarot Card: The Hermit – being a shining light for all of life

Gemstones: Emerald, malachite, sapphire

Plant Remedy: Sagebrush – the ability to hold and store light

Fragrance: Lavender – management and storage of energy

new Moon in Virgo

September 5, 4:37 AM

Virgo Challenges and Victories

Today I recognize what I love most about myself. I am the source of my love, my life, and my experience. I will set aside time today to nurture myself. I allow myself to receive these gifts and know in my heart that it is natural for me to love myself. I discover, deep within myself, the knowing that the love I give myself is commensurate to the love I am willing to receive from others. I am aware that what I expect from others cannot be truly expressed or experienced if I cannot give to myself first. I can never be disappointed when I know that love is a natural resource for me today.

Today, I honor the Earth by acknowledging what she has given me. I take time out to walk in the woods or on the beach, to feel the power of the creative pulse of the creative forces flowing through my body with the energy of being alive. I spend time in my garden and plant flowers to enhance the idea of beauty today. I honor my body today and get a massage. I spend quality time sharing joyful moments with those who love to connect from the heart and realize the blessings that come from living my life with love.

Virgo Homework

Virgo co-creates best through working with herbology, folk medicine, environmental industries, organic farming, recycling, horticulture, acupuncture, healing arts, nutritional counseling, yoga instruction, and editing.

The Virgo moon cycle gives birth to Divinity in its own unique way, understanding the Soul's blueprint to be a temple of beauty. This creates what is known as the "crisis of perfection" within the minds of mankind during this time. We become aware of Spirit ascending and descending at the same time and must recognize that these contradicting energies are working within us in order to give birth to Divinity.

New Moon in Virgo

September 5, 4:37 AM

Five Steps to Co-Creation

1. Acceptance

Acceptance opens the pathway to living in the moment and makes way for opportunity to occur. Co-creation can only occur when you live in the moment.

Start your list by writing... "I accept _____ into my life."

2. Adjustment

Consider what adjustments you may need to make in order to receive what you are accepting into your life.

My Co-Creation List

new Moon in Virgo

September 5, 4:37 AM

3. Awakening

Once your list is complete, use the power of sound and read your list out loud. This directs your intentions (your list) toward actualization and co-creation.

4. Alignment

Now it is time to make a petition to the Universe, using these words, "I call on the power of the Universe to know I am ready to receive my list. I accept it. I allow it. So be it! This, or something better than this, comes to me in an easy and pleasurable way for the good of all concerned. Thank You Universe!" Light your candle and place it on your eight-sided mirror.

5. Acknowledgement

When a creation result is acknowledged it seals the deal. This makes room for more magnificence to expand into your life and increases your abundance factor adding to your ability to receive.

As each aspect of your co-creation list arrives in your life, spend time allowing, acknowledging, and accepting it with the true gusto of gratitude. You might want to make a victory list here.

Victory List

Virgo Questions to ask Myself

Where am I best at finding Divinity in the details?

Where do I tend to create a crisis of perfection?

How can I accept that all my experiences lead to higher awareness?

new Moon in Virgo

September 5, 4:37 AM

How to Use the Moon Book With Your Chart

Fill in the blanks on the Cosmic Check-In page. Then look up the degree of the moon on the chart below. Take note of the "I" statement on the outside of the wheel where the moon is located. Now locate the same degree on your own chart, and make a note of the house and corresponding "I" statement. Go back to the Cosmic Check-In page and circle the two statements from the charts and read what you wrote. This will give you an idea about what to expect from this moon phase on a personal level.

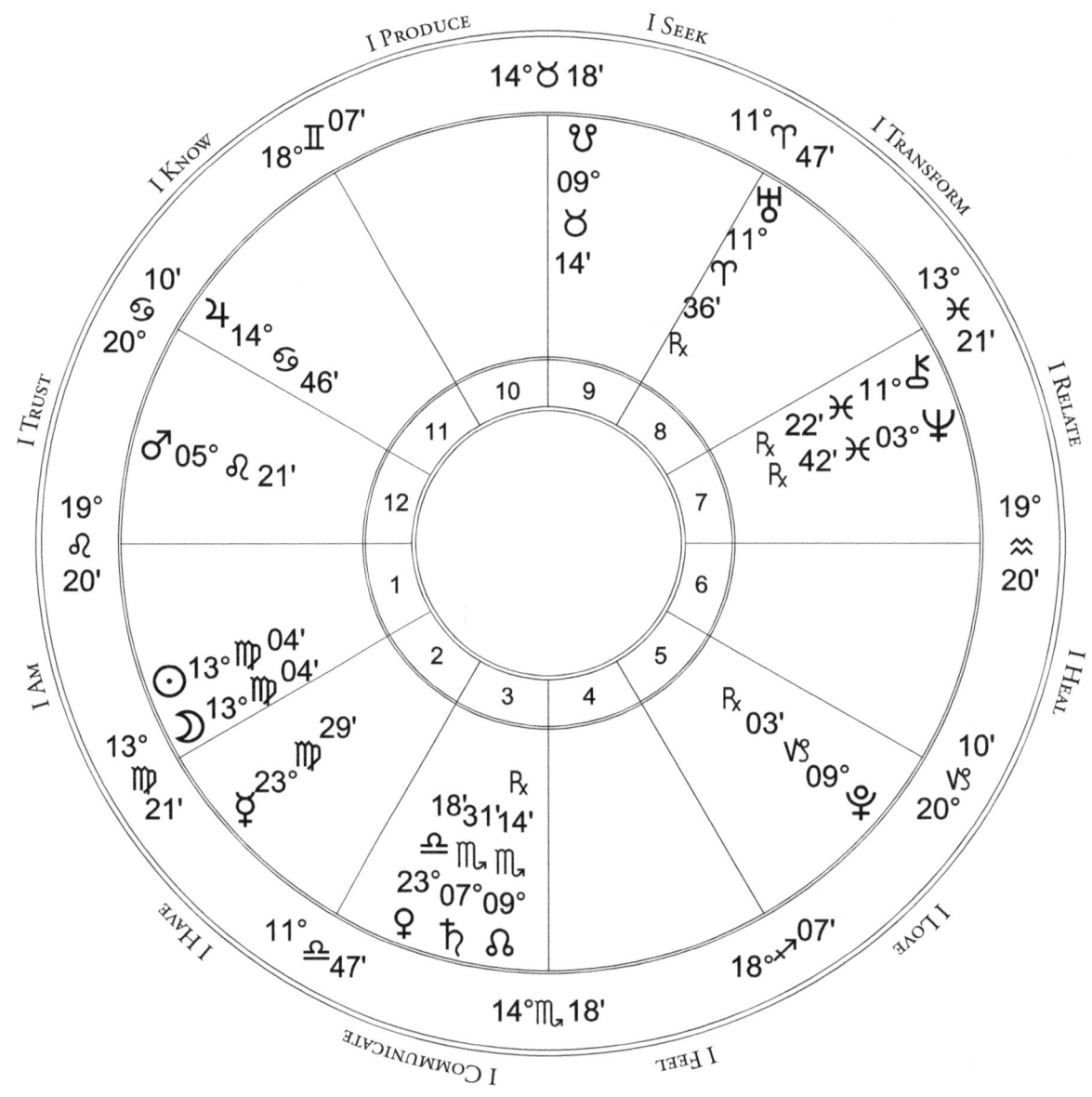

♈ Aries	♋ Cancer	♏ Scorpio	♓ Pisces	♀ Venus	♅ Uranus	☊ North Node
♉ Taurus	♌ Leo	♐ Sagittarius	☉ Sun	♂ Mars	♆ Neptune	☋ South Node
♊ Gemini	♍ Virgo	♑ Capricorn	☽ Moon	♃ Jupiter	♀ or ♇ Pluto	℞ Retrograde
	♎ Libra	♒ Aquarius	☿ Mercury	♄ Saturn	⚷ Chiron	

162

new Moon in Virgo

September 5, 4:37 AM

Cosmic Check-In

Take a moment to write a brief phrase for each "I" statement.
This activates all areas of your life for this creative cycle.

♍ I Heal

♎ I Relate

♏ I Transform

♐ I Seek

♑ I Produce

♒ I Know

♓ I Trust

♈ I Am

♉ I Have

♊ I Communicate

♋ I Feel

♌ I Love

Full Moon in Pisces

September 19, 4:14 AM

Statement I Trust
Body Feet
Mind Super-sensitive
Spirit Mystical

The Sun is Opposite the Moon

Full Moons are always in opposition to the Sun. This creates a feeling of tension between where you want to shine and how your feelings are flowing on a sensory level about the Sun's directive. The two forces seem like they are working against each other, yet they are on the same team displaying different techniques to attain the same mission. The Pisces/Virgo polarity creates tension between addiction and perfection.

Pisces Goddess

The Pisces goddess, Kuan Yin, is the embodiment of all that is compassionate. She guides us to the abyss, a place known as the "Great Unknown." It is here that the ego drops away and there is only the truth of one's nature. Kuan Yin protects us and holds us when we let go, surrender, and evolve. She is the Goddess of Emptiness and helps us to constantly empty the self from the limitations of the ego: fear, doubt, guilt, shame, and denial. In exchange, we gain beauty, light, and service. She is often pictured riding on the head of a dragon. It is the breath of the dragon that pierces the veil of the illusion.

Pisces Freedom List Ideas

Now is the time to free myself from…

- Addictions
- Illusions and fantasy
- Escape dramas
- Martyrdom
- Victimhood
- Mental chaos

On Your Altar

Colors: Greens, blues, amethyst, aquamarine

Numerology: 2 – Balance logic with intuition

Tarot card: The Hanged Man – learning to let go

Gemstones: Opal, turquoise, amethyst

Plant Remedy: Passion flower – the ability to live in the here and now

Fragrance: White lotus – connecting to the divine without arrogance

Full Moon in Pisces

September 19, 4:14 AM

Memory Maintenance Meditation

The Moon governs our memory and the maintenance of our memory. It is our memory that often creates blocks to setting us free to be able to attain our goals. The Moon works with us to help us become free from memory blocks three days after the Full Moon. The freedom themes are provided by the zodiac sign and can be from this lifetime or other lifetimes. These meditations assist in dissolving blocks and open pathways to new frontiers.

When the Moon is in Pisces, take time out to sit quietly. Close your eyes and breathe in and out. Ask the Angel of Records to go with you to see the chaotic regions in the matrix of your mind. See your hidden desires. Look with the eye of compassion to understand where these desires have hurt you or others. Expect a major healing by asking for grace to be given to you while visiting these sordid versions of your past. Make amends with yourself for romanticizing your past and release any escape fantasies that keep you from being present with yourself and with life. Allow yourself to be ignited with your power to heal. Visit hospitals and prisons; offer healings. Focus on your creative, spiritual self.

Pisces Challenges and Victories

The best thing I can do for myself today is to get out of the way, so life can take its own course without the interference of my control drama. I take time out to let go and let things be. I have become too involved in the details and have lost sight of the vastness of the Universe and the infinite possibilities that are available to me at all times and in every moment. I am aware that all I need is a different way of seeing what I have perceived as a problem, and that my view is limited by my needs rather than by accepting things as they are. I trust that, when I get out of the way and give space to the power of NOW, all is in Divine Order and everything works out for the good of all concerned. This is the day when doing nothing, gets me everything. I allow myself to experience the void. I empty myself of my rigidity, small-mindedness, racing thoughts, the need to be right, and to control outcomes. I know that non-action will present me with right action. I give God a chance and trust the view to be larger than mine. When I accept myself as I am, I learn what I can become. I remove myself from all of the mind chatter and allow for silence to do its work. I am aware that a quiet mind brings me peace (the absence of conflict). In turning upside down, I see how right-side-up things really are. Acceptance brings me perspective. Acceptance sets me free. Acceptance brings me wholeness. Acceptance widens my mind.

Pisces Homework

Get a foot massage to bring your energy back to the ground. Feel the power of your path on the bottom of your feet. Now that you are back to your body, it is time to make a list of the ways your boundaries get breached. After the completion of your list, read it out loud and then throw it in the ocean. Now it is time to see the seed of life, the seed of love, and the seed of power that was planted into the womb of evolution.

Full Moon in Pisces

September 19, 4:14 AM

Five Steps to Freedom

When we work with the concept of freedom we are soon presented with resistance. Freedom presents a pathway for us to bump directly into our limitations. When we can become aware of these limits, we can then find our way to freedom. Below are some ideas that might assist you in seeing deeper into your resistance to accepting freedom into your life. Once you discover these you might want to add more to your freedom list.

1. Feeling Useless

This happens when you measure yourself by what others think of you.

2. Discouragement

This occurs when you use blame others instead of taking responsibility for your part in a situation.

3. Regret

This happens when you live inside past events and continue to rehearse your story, hoping that if you tell it enough, it will get resolved. Living in the past leads to regret and blocks you from freedom.

4. Limitation

This happens when we think that there is no way out of a challenge, which creates an inability to see options. When options are out of the picture we become unable to create positive outcomes.

5. Self-Doubt

This takes place when we think that others are better than we are. Growing cannot occur when we have given someone else our ceiling.

Full Moon in Pisces

September 19, 4:14 AM

My Freedom List

Pisces Questions to Ask Myself

What is my addiction?

How does my addiction get activated?

What am I putting off so I can continue to escape from reality?

Full Moon in Pisces

September 19, 4:14 AM

How to Use the Moon Book With Your Chart

Fill in the blanks on the Cosmic Check-In page. Then look up the degree of the moon on the chart below. Take note of the "I" statement on the outside of the wheel where the moon is located. Now locate the same degree on your own chart, and make a note of the house and corresponding "I" statement. Go back to the Cosmic Check-In page and circle the two statements from the charts and read what you wrote. This will give you an idea about what to expect from this moon phase on a personal level.

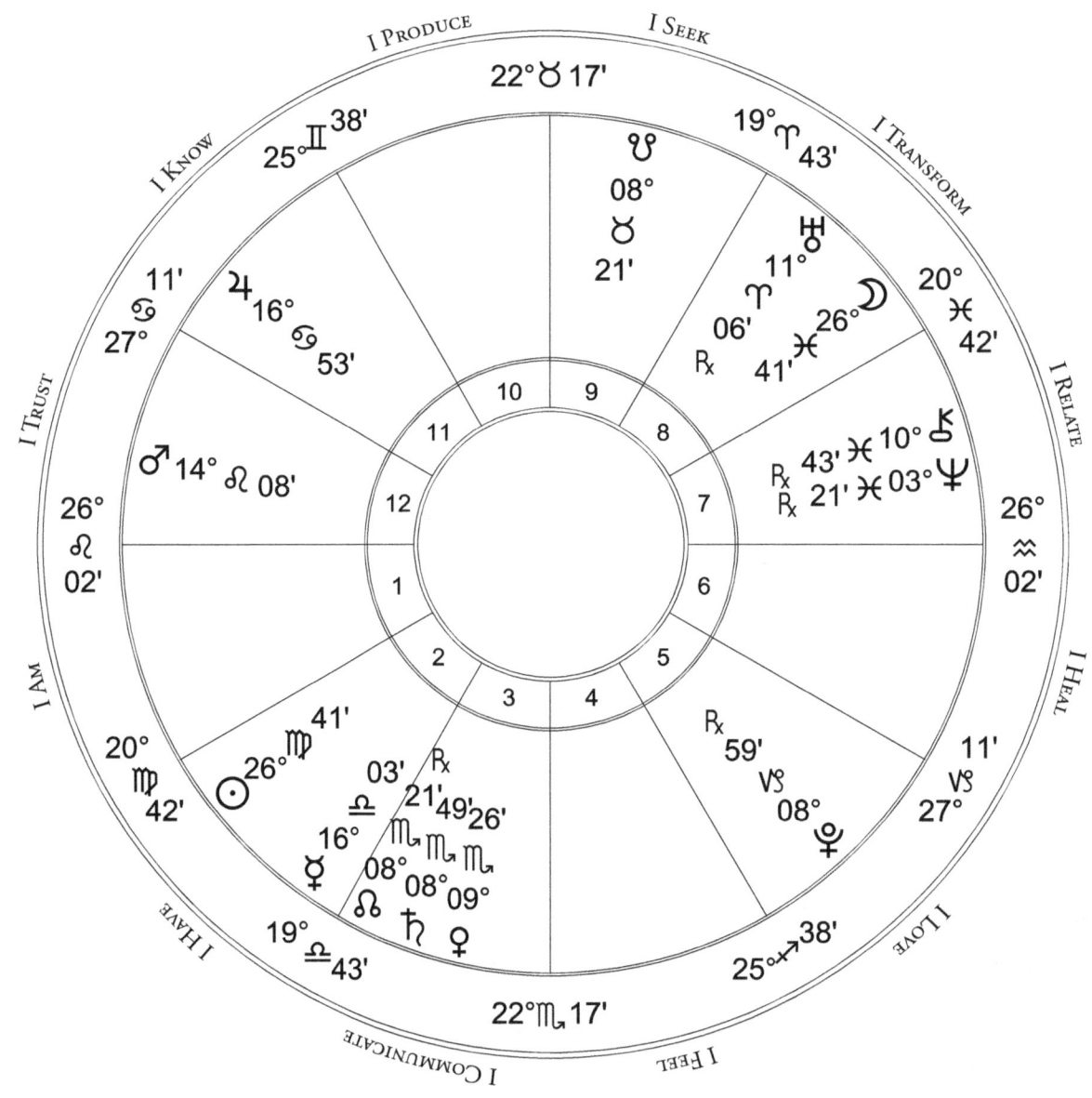

♈ Aries	♋ Cancer	♏ Scorpio	♓ Pisces	♀ Venus	♅ Uranus	☊ North Node
♉ Taurus	♌ Leo	♐ Sagittarius	☉ Sun	♂ Mars	♆ Neptune	☋ South Node
♊ Gemini	♍ Virgo	♑ Capricorn	☽ Moon	♃ Jupiter	♀ or ♇ Pluto	℞ Retrograde
	♎ Libra	♒ Aquarius	☿ Mercury	♄ Saturn	⚷ Chiron	

full Moon in Pisces

September 19, 4:14 AM

Cosmic Check-In

Take a moment to write a brief phrase for each "I" statement.
This activates all areas of your life for this freedom cycle.

♓ I Trust

♈ I Am

♉ I Have

♊ I Communicate

♋ I Feel

♌ I Love

♍ I Heal

♎ I Relate

♏ I Transform

♐ I Seek

♑ I Produce

♒ I Know

October 2013

SUN	MON	TUE	WED	THU	FRI	SAT
		1 ΨℍδℝR ☽ → ♍ 11:53 AM 5. A change of attitude can change your outcome.	**2** ΨℍδℝR 6. Invite someone to dine in your home.	**3** ΨℍδℝR ☽ V/C 11:58 AM ☽ → ♎ 8:00 PM 7. Your inner wisdom can inspire others.	**4** ΨℍδℝR ● 11°♎56' 5:36 PM 8. Visualize a challenge being over.	**5** ΨℍδℝR ☽ V/C 3:29 PM 9. The light you shine today never goes away.
6 ΨℍδℝR ☽ → ♏ 1:34 AM 10. You can change a troubled past.	**7** ΨℍδℝR ♀ → ♐ 10:55 AM ☽ V/C 9:55 PM 2. When you are balanced, life flourishes.	**8** ΨℍδℝR ☽ → ♐ 5:22 AM 3. Your creativity can bring you peace.	**9** ΨℍδℝR ▲ 4. With pure intent, miracles happen.	**10** ΨℍδℝR ▲ ☽ V/C 3:12 AM ☽ → ♑ 8:18 AM 5. Redefine your DNA by dropping negativity.	**11** ΨℍδℝR ☽ V/C 5:05 PM 6. Love of others comes in love of self.	**12** ΨℍδℝR ☽ → ♒ 11:01 AM 7. Move beyond sound bites for information.
13 ΨℍδℝR 8. There are no limits to what you can do.	**14** ΨℍδℝR Columbus Day ☽ V/C 1:29 PM ☽ → ♓ 2:07 PM 9. Ask Spirit for guidance.	**15** ΨℍδℝR ♂ → ♍ 4:06 AM 10. Feeling peace makes a future bright.	**16** ΨℍδℝR ☽ V/C 12:16 AM ☽ → ♈ 6:19 PM 2. Work side-by-side in harmony.	**17** ΨℍδℝR 3. You are a marvel of creation.	**18** ΨℍδℝR ◯ 25°♈51' 4:39 PM Lunar Eclipse 4:51 PM ☽ V/C 4:39 PM 4. Know that others count on you.	**19** ΨℍδℝR ☽ → ♉ 12:28 AM 5. Find a pace that is best for you.
20 ΨℍδℝR ☽ V/C 2:03 PM 7. You will always know what to do.	**21** ♀ΨℍδℝR ♀R-18°♏23' 3:30 AM ☽ → ♊ 9:15 AM 8. We all have different tasks on Earth.	**22** ♀ΨℍδℝR ▼ ☽ V/C 5:36 PM ☉ → ♏ 11:11 PM 9. Know you are loved without measure.	**23** ♀ΨℍδℝR ▼ ☽ → ♋ 8:37 PM 10. Your future does not include the past.	**24** ♀ΨℍδℝR 2. Know you are in partnership with the planet.	**25** ♀ΨℍδℝR ☽ V/C 1:32 PM 3. Above all, be true to yourself.	**26** ♀ΨℍδℝR ☽ → ♌ 9:13 AM 4. Choose to learn from your experiences.
27 ♀ΨℍδℝR 5. Nothing happens until you act.	**28** ♀ΨℍδℝR ☽ V/C 5:27 AM ☽ → ♍ 8:46 PM 6. Listen to another's point of view.	**29** ♀ΨℍδℝR 7. Think before you act.	**30** ♀ΨℍδℝR ☽ V/C 7:49 PM 8. The Universe rewards your efforts.	**31** ♀ΨℍδℝR Halloween ☽ → ♎ 5:23 AM 9. Reinforce your prayers with action.		

October 2013 Planetary Highlights

Neptune Retrograde in Pisces for the Entire Month

Look where you keep yourself in denial around anything that seems to be realistic in any way, shape, or form. You may feel uncomfortable and start setting the stage for some escape dramas.

Uranus is Retrograde in Aries for the Entire Month

Do what you can to see how often you balk over having to do what makes someone else happy rather than making yourself happy. Take a good look at how unhappy you can make yourself feel when you don't get your way. Uranus loves chaos and rebellion and Aries love a battlefield, it is your choice how to make this work.

Chiron is Retrograde in Pisces for the Entire Month

Take time out each day this month to partake in a method of healing; maybe a yoga class or Sufi dancing. Join a meditation group and practice magnetizing silence to lessen the stress in your life. Take a class all about the religions of the world and see if you can find a thread of truth in each one you learn about.

Mercury goes Retrograde in Scorpio – October 21, 3:30 AM

Get ready for hard edged communication. It could be quite damaging if the person you are talking to has a storage bin of undelivered feelings or secrets. Remember, the bowels of the Earth need to talk too and it could be slimy. Best to keep conversations light and all about the moment in order to make it through this one.

October 4 – Mercury and Saturn Meet Up

Expect a powerful testing ground to occur between the mind and the ability to use thought. This could be rough around the edges if the mind feels challenged and has to defend itself. Make use of your thoughts by staying focused on the high road. The best use of this pattern is to take on a research project. Avoid blame and stay accountable.

October 4 – The Sun and Moon in Libra are Opposing Uranus Retrograde in Aries

The Sun's directive with Uranus' ideas here could lead to a breakthrough invention that actually can be channeled right into the marketplace by Libra's charm and the moon's germination abilities. Go for it!

October 7, 10:55 AM – Venus enters Sagittarius

Expect to play hard and play fast. Love, money, luxury, and adventure are in the mix. Enjoy it while it lasts.

October 15, 4:06 AM – Mars enters Virgo

Virgo likes small places and Mars likes expansion. Expect a squelching, inhibiting feeling to happen. The critical complaining mind of Virgo could make one a bit unpopular right now. If you keep Mars' high energy in the body, a major recalibration could happen adding a new dimension to your body maintenance program. Use it!

October 22, 11:11 PM – The Sun enters Scorpio

This is a time when all of Nature is dying and going underground. Transformation is available in the Spring. It's time to rejuvenate and let the sojourn below the surface embrace you into knowing yourself better. Discover what you have kept hidden, even from yourself, and bring back some rewards to share with others.

October 9 and 10 – Super-Sensitivity ▲

Depression can be running through the atmosphere at this time based on an inability for decisions that need to be made globally. A stalled process is occurring based on an imbalance due to resistance that could be very annoying. Do what you can to stay out of it.

October 22 and 23 – Low-Vitality ▼

Some underground process, under the Earth, is creating a weakness and leaving us exhausted. To avoid a personal overload, it is best to stay out of it, even on a thinking basis. Get rest and stay close to home.

♈ Aries	♋ Cancer	♐ Sagittarius	☽ Moon	♄ Saturn	☊ North Node	V/C Void-of-Course
♉ Taurus	♌ Leo	♑ Capricorn	☿ Mercury	♅ Uranus	☋ South Node	▲ Super-Sensitivity
♊ Gemini	♍ Virgo	♒ Aquarius	♀ Venus	♆ Neptune	➡ Enters	▼ Low-Vitality
	♎ Libra	♓ Pisces	♂ Mars	♀ or ♇ Pluto	℞ Retrograde	
	♏ Scorpio	☉ Sun	♃ Jupiter	⚷ Chiron	S/D Stationary Direct	

New Moon in Libra

October 4, 5:36 PM

Statement I Relate
Body Kidneys
Mind Social
Spirit Harmony

When the Sun is in Libra

Libra energy gives us the opportunity to bridge the gap between the higher and lower mind; abstract thinking versus concrete thinking. During Libra time, the light and dark forces are in balance and we are given a chance to experience harmony. Harmony occurs when we keep our polarities in motion and put paradox to rest, thus breaking the crystallization of polarity. Now is the time to weigh our values through the light of our soul. Libra asks us to look at what is increasing and decreasing in our lives. Start with friendship, courage, sincerity, and understanding, and keep going until your scale is in motion.

Libra Goddess

The whole idea of Libra is to weigh and measure decreasing and increasing light. The goddess best known for the ability to measure light is Ma'at. Ma'at has the ability to weigh and measure frequencies of a light heart or a heavy one. According to Egyptian mythology, it is Ma'at who waits at the gateway to the other side and measures the lightness of being in order to determine the direction one is to take when entering the Underworld. Ma'at's symbol for measurement is an ostrich plume. Each heart that enters must be weighed and be in balance against her feather. If the heart is heavy, it is determined by Ma'at that the soul must transition to an area known as the darker world. If the heart is light and balanced with her feather, the soul is directed to the lighter world. Because of this process, she began to make her contribution to civilization by holding the space for cosmic balance, right order, and natural law.

Libra Co-Creation Ideas

Now is the time to focus on...

- Relationships
- Wholeness
- Being loving, lovable, and loved
- Living life as an art form
- Balance and equality
- Integrity
- Accuracy
- Diplomacy
- Peace

On Your Altar

Colors: Pink, green

Numerology: 8 – The ability to make life successful

Tarot Card: Justice – the Law of Cause and Effect

Gemstones: Jade, rose quartz

Plant Remedy: Olive Trees – stamina

Fragrance: Eucalyptus – clarity of breath

new Moon in Libra

October 4, 5:36 PM

Libra Challenges and Victories

I feel the call of the higher worlds awakening me to a new vibration. This call is to move beyond judgment and move to a place of acceptance, understanding, unconditional confidence, and love. I am at a place in my life where I can embrace the world of acceptance and wholeness because I have birthed myself anew, beyond the imprisonment and crystallization of polarity and righteousness. My black and white worlds of right and wrong have integrated and blended into gray, the color of wisdom, where true knowledge exists. Knowledge simply is, and the need for proof does not exist where wisdom lives.

The only requirement is experience. I know that everything that comes before me is a direct reflection of my own experience and, in embracing this concept, I can now receive the gift of infinite awareness. I am in a place of awareness that came before and goes beyond where good and evil existed. I have within me, the presence of unconditional confidence to go where true love lives. I no longer need to prove myself. I am now simply being myself. I release the need to be right and accept the right to BE. I no longer need to be forgiven because I am not wrong nor right. I no longer need to define myself. Acceptance has no reason for defense. I no longer need to be guilty; duty motivation is no longer a reality. I know that where there is judgment, there is separation. I know understanding unifies. I accept the call of the higher worlds and express myself freely and fully without fear of judgment. I accept myself as I am so I can learn what I can become.

Libra Homework

Libra co-creates best through the legal industry, beauty industry, diplomatic service, match-making, urban development, mediation, feng shui, spa ownership, clutter busting and space clearing, romance writing, wedding consulting, fashion design, and as a librarian.

It is time to weigh and measure the values of relationship, friendship, courage, sensitivity, sincerity, and understanding. Look at what is increasing and what is decreasing in these areas.

New Moon in Libra

October 4, 5:36 PM

Five Steps to Co-Creation

1. Acceptance

Acceptance opens the pathway to living in the moment and makes way for opportunity to occur. Co-creation can only occur when you live in the moment.

Start your list by writing... "I accept _____ into my life."

2. Adjustment

Consider what adjustments you may need to make in order to receive what you are accepting into your life.

My Co-Creation List

New Moon in Libra

October 4, 5:36 PM

3. Awakening

Once your list is complete, use the power of sound and read your list out loud. This directs your intentions (your list) toward actualization and co-creation.

4. Alignment

Now it is time to make a petition to the Universe, using these words, "I call on the power of the Universe to know I am ready to receive my list. I accept it. I allow it. So be it! This, or something better than this, comes to me in an easy and pleasurable way for the good of all concerned. Thank You Universe!" Light your candle and place it on your eight-sided mirror.

5. Acknowledgement

When a creation result is acknowledged it seals the deal. This makes room for more magnificence to expand into your life and increases your abundance factor adding to your ability to receive.

As each aspect of your co-creation list arrives in your life, spend time allowing, acknowledging, and accepting it with the true gusto of gratitude. You might want to make a victory list here.

Victory List

Libra Questions to ask Myself

Where am I wasting my time by thinking, rather than being?

What can I do to stop defending my position?

How can I become one with the Infinite Presence and find bliss?

new Moon in Libra

October 4, 5:36 PM

How to Use the Moon Book With Your Chart

Fill in the blanks on the Cosmic Check-In page. Then look up the degree of the moon on the chart below. Take note of the "I" statement on the outside of the wheel where the moon is located. Now locate the same degree on your own chart, and make a note of the house and corresponding "I" statement. Go back to the Cosmic Check-In page and circle the two statements from the charts and read what you wrote. This will give you an idea about what to expect from this moon phase on a personal level.

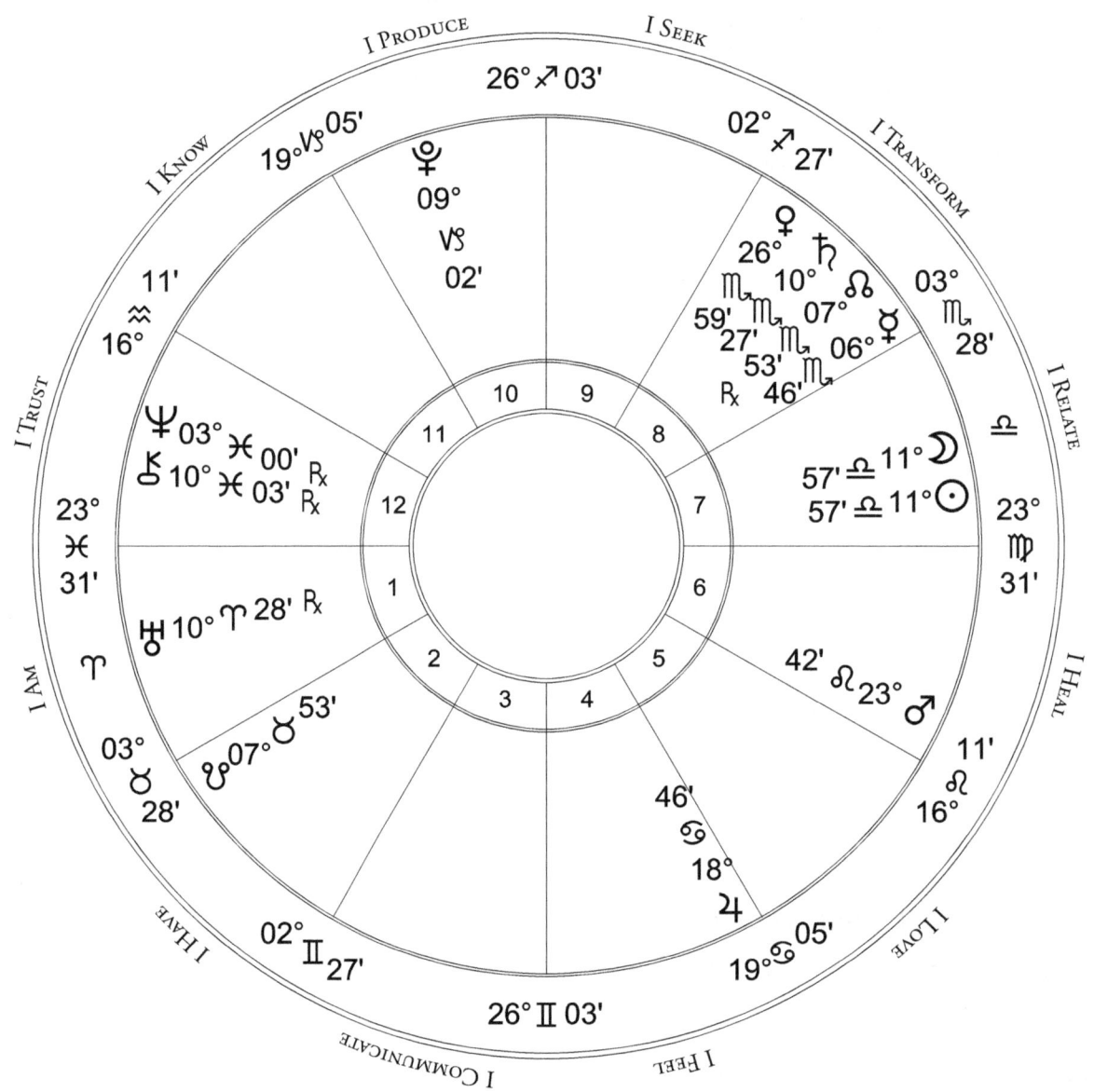

♈ Aries	♋ Cancer	♏ Scorpio	♓ Pisces	♀ Venus	♅ Uranus	☊ North Node
♉ Taurus	♌ Leo	♐ Sagittarius	☉ Sun	♂ Mars	♆ Neptune	☋ South Node
♊ Gemini	♍ Virgo	♑ Capricorn	☽ Moon	♃ Jupiter	♀ or ♇ Pluto	℞ Retrograde
	♎ Libra	♒ Aquarius	☿ Mercury	♄ Saturn	⚷ Chiron	

new Moon in Libra

October 4, 5:36 PM

Cosmic Check-In

Take a moment to write a brief phrase for each "I" statement.
This activates all areas of your life for this creative cycle.

♎ I Relate

♏ I Transform

♐ I Seek

♑ I Produce

♒ I Know

♓ I Trust

♈ I Am

♉ I Have

♊ I Communicate

♋ I Feel

♌ I Love

♍ I Heal

Full Moon in Aries

October 18, 4:39 PM

Statement I Am
Body Head
Mind Impulsive
Spirit Initiation

The Sun is Opposite the Moon

Full Moons are always in opposition to the Sun. This creates a feeling of tension between where you want to shine and how your feelings are flowing on a sensory level about the Sun's directive. The two forces seem like they are working against each other, yet they are on the same team displaying different techniques to attain the same goal. The Aries/Libra polarity creates tension between "I Am" and "We Are."

Aries God

Mars is the God of War. His statement is, "I fight." Before going into battle, Mars required something to be sacrificed on the eve of the battle. When he went into battle, he traveled with two goddesses: Deimous, Goddess of Terror, and Phobos, Goddess of Fear. They symbolized the unconscious elements of war. It never mattered to Mars on which side of the war he fought; it was the battle itself that seduced him. When the Moon is full in Aries, we are given the opportunity to examine the inner conflict. Where are we at war with our Self, our relationships, and our environment? Questions to ask yourself: Is my anger worth the sacrifice? What am I sacrificing in order to stay angry?

Aries Freedom List Ideas

Now is the time to free myself from...

- Anger that is toxic
- Competition and comparison
- Irritation and struggle
- The need to be first
- Overdoing it, without rest
- Impatience
- Impulsiveness
- Challenge and hostility

On Your Altar

Colors: Red, black, coral

Numerology: 4 – Re-translate structure

Tarot Card: Tower – release from a stuck place, a major breakthrough

Gemstones: Diamond, red jasper, coral, obsidian

Plant Remedy: Oak, pomegranate – planting new life and rooting new life

Fragrance: Ginger – the ability to ingest and digest life

Full Moon in Aries

October 18, 4:39 PM

Memory Maintenance Meditation

The Moon governs our memory and the maintenance of our memory. It is our memory that often creates blocks to setting us free to be able to attain our goals. The Moon works with us to help us become free from memory blocks three days after the Full Moon. The freedom themes are provided by the zodiac sign and can be from this lifetime or other lifetimes. These meditations assist in dissolving blocks and open pathways to new frontiers.

When the Moon is in Aries, it is a time to face irritability issues relating to challenge, hostility, impatience, and war. Sit quietly and close your eyes, breathe in and breathe out and look in the memory banks for times when you forced your will on others, and reconcile with the old warrior that you were. Open the pathway to becoming the peaceful warrior who expresses without impatience or the impulse of battle. Take action, be energized, and focus on yourself. Know that you have the power to work things out with clear self-expression. Continue to see yourself clearly, without the interfering definitions of others.

Aries Challenges and Victories

Today, I let go. I trust that whatever breaks down or breaks through is a blessing in disguise for me. I make a commitment to allow myself to be spontaneous and live in the moment. I know the unexpected is a blessing for me and a way for me to make a breakthrough out of my limitations. I am aware that I am resistant to change. I know I must make changes and am too stubborn to take the appropriate action myself to change. I have built many walls of false protection around me, guarding me and blocking me from the reality that change is a constant. I have freeze-framed my life and desire support to update myself. I have allowed my fear of change to become my false motto and my life is at a standstill. I am unwilling use any more energy to perpetuate my resistance. I know that continuing to cling to the past is a waste of my energy. I can no longer put things off that delay my process. I feel the breaking down of form. I trust that all changes are in my favor. All changes lead me to golden opportunities. I release false pride. I release false foundations. I release false authorities. In so doing, I allow for everything to crumble around me so I can see that my true strength is within and I will build my life from the inside out.

I am ready for new experiences. I am ready for the unexpected. I am willing to have an event occur so I can become activated towards my breakthrough. I am ready for the power of now. I know being spontaneous will bring me to true joy. I know if I ride this carrier wave it will take me to a place far beyond my scope of limited thinking. I know the will of God works in my favor and knows more than I do in any given moment.

Aries Homework

Now you are ready to take a personal inventory on behaviors such as impatience, talking over people, brat attacks, and starting every sentence with "I."

This is a time when the light becomes a prisoner of polarized forces. This diminishing light begins its yearly sojourn beneath the surface asking us to balance light and dark by mastering the concept of equilibrium. Equilibrium is the Law of Harmony, where we attempt to reach a state of achievement by combining paradoxical fields that break the crystallization of polarity. Spend time looking for increasing and decreasing fields of light around you.

full Moon in Aries

October 18, 4:39 PM

Five Steps to Freedom

When we work with the concept of freedom we are soon presented with resistance. Freedom presents a pathway for us to bump directly into our limitations. When we can become aware of these limits, we can then find our way to freedom. Below are some ideas that might assist you in seeing deeper into your resistance to accepting freedom into your life. Once you discover these you might want to add more to your freedom list.

1. Feeling Useless

This happens when you measure yourself by what others think of you.

2. Discouragement

This occurs when you use blame others instead of taking responsibility for your part in a situation.

3. Regret

This happens when you live inside past events and continue to rehearse your story, hoping that if you tell it enough, it will get resolved. Living in the past leads to regret and blocks you from freedom.

4. Limitation

This happens when we think that there is no way out of a challenge, which creates an inability to see options. When options are out of the picture we become unable to create positive outcomes.

5. Self-Doubt

This takes place when we think that others are better than we are. Growing cannot occur when we have given someone else our ceiling.

full Moon in Aries

October 18, 4:39 PM

My Freedom List

Aries Questions to Ask Myself

In what area do I seem to be the most competitive?

How can I get the positive recognition I so deeply desire?

What can I do to curb my impatience?

full Moon in Aries

October 18, 4:39 PM

How to Use the Moon Book With Your Chart

Fill in the blanks on the Cosmic Check-In page. Then look up the degree of the moon on the chart below. Take note of the "I" statement on the outside of the wheel where the moon is located. Now locate the same degree on your own chart, and make a note of the house and corresponding "I" statement. Go back to the Cosmic Check-In page and circle the two statements from the charts and read what you wrote. This will give you an idea about what to expect from this moon phase on a personal level.

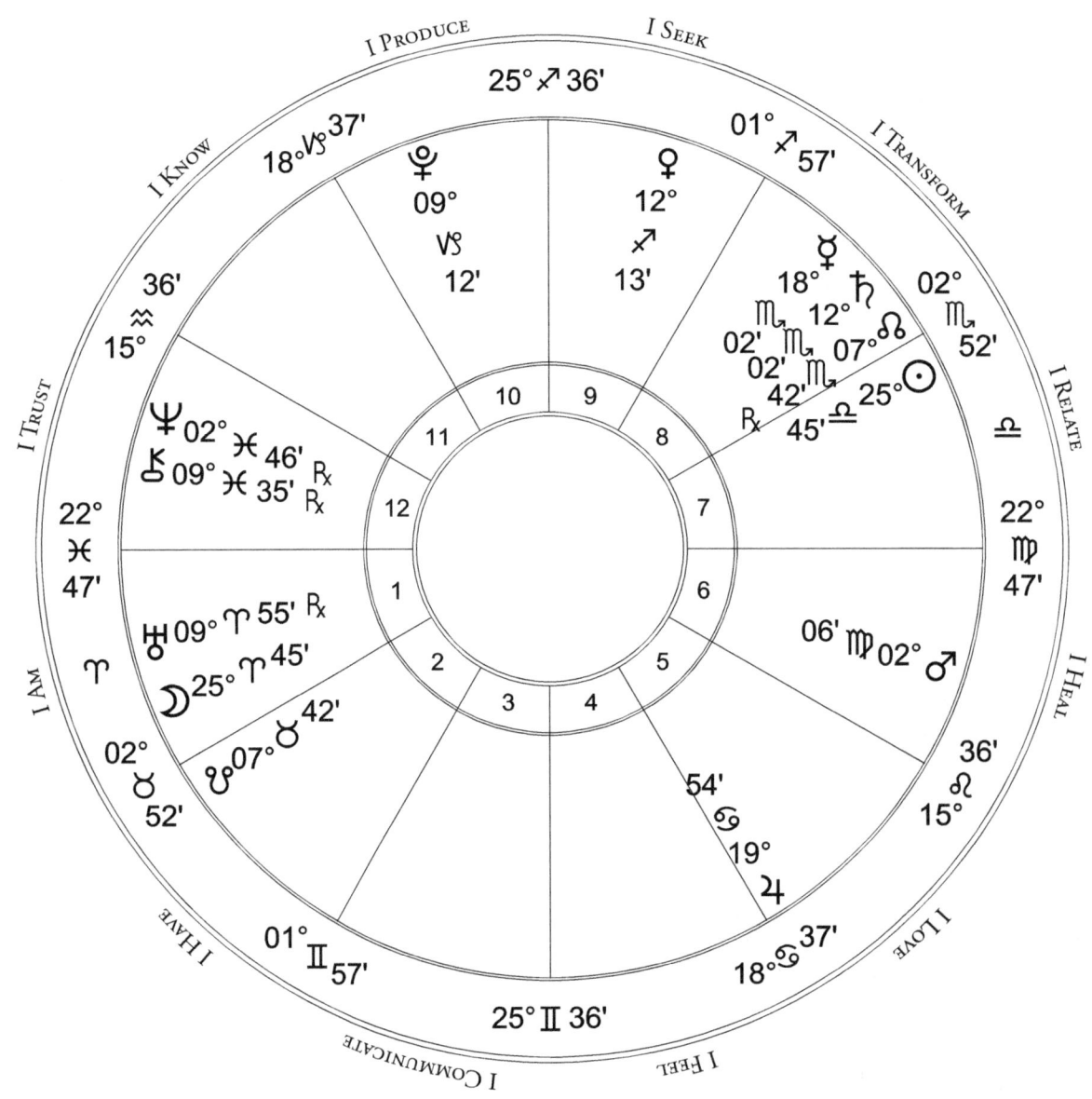

♈ Aries	♋ Cancer	♏ Scorpio	♓ Pisces	♀ Venus	♅ Uranus	☊ North Node
♉ Taurus	♌ Leo	♐ Sagittarius	☉ Sun	♂ Mars	♆ Neptune	☋ South Node
♊ Gemini	♍ Virgo	♑ Capricorn	☽ Moon	♃ Jupiter	♀ or ♇ Pluto	℞ Retrograde
	♎ Libra	♒ Aquarius	☿ Mercury	♄ Saturn	⚷ Chiron	

full Moon in Aries

October 18, 4:39 PM

Cosmic Check-In

Take a moment to write a brief phrase for each "I" statement.
This activates all areas of your life for this freedom cycle.

♈ I Am

♉ I Have

♊ I Communicate

♋ I Feel

♌ I Love

♍ I Heal

♎ I Relate

♏ I Transform

♐ I Seek

♑ I Produce

♒ I Know

♓ I Trust

November 2013

SUN	MON	TUE	WED	THU	FRI	SAT
					1 ☿♆♅⚷℞ 10. Move forward with grace and ease.	**2** ☿♆♅⚷℞ ☽ V/C 5:48 AM ☽ → ♏ 10:36 AM 2. Being adaptable creates harmony.
3 ☿♆♅⚷℞ ● 11°♏16′ 4:51 AM Solar Eclipse 4:47 AM PST BEGINS ☽ V/C 8:24 PM 3. Express your artistic nature.	**4** ☿♆♅⚷℞ ☽ → ♐ 12:15 PM 4. A practical approach stabilizes energy.	**5** ☿♆♅⚷℞▲ ♀ → ♑ 12:44 AM ☽ V/C 8:49 AM 5. Adaptability sets you free.	**6** ☿♃♆♅⚷℞▲ ♃℞-20°♋30′ 9:04 PM ☽ → ♑ 1:45 PM 6. Know that you are dearly loved.	**7** ☿♃♆♅⚷℞ ☽ V/C 11:40 PM 7. Curiosity stimulates you mentally.	**8** ☿♃♆♅⚷℞ ☽ → ♒ 3:31 PM 8. Being practical gives you power.	**9** ☿♃♆♅⚷℞ ☽ V/C 9:58 PM 9. Spirit rewards you with just the right answers.
10 ♃♆♅⚷℞ ☿D - 2°♏30′ 1:13 PM ☽ → ♓ 6:37 PM 10. Cyclic time frees you from linear constraints.	**11** ♃♆♅⚷℞ Veteran's Day 2. Closure may require forgiveness.	**12** ♃♆♅⚷℞ ☽ V/C 6:35 AM ☽ → ♈ 11:40 PM 3. Live joyfully in the moment.	**13** ♃♅⚷℞ ♆D - 2°♓34′ 10:43 AM 4. Be patient with yourself and others.	**14** ♃♅⚷℞ ☽ V/C 12:58 PM 5. Make no changes out of fear.	**15** ♃♅⚷℞ ☽ → ♉ 6:50 AM 6. Tolerance and understanding generate love.	**16** ♃♅⚷℞ 7. Learn something new about technology.
17 ♃♅⚷℞ ○ 25°♉26′ 7:17 AM ☽ V/C 7:17 AM ☽ → ♊ 4:08 PM 8. Celebrate your abundance.	**18** ♃♅⚷℞ 9. There is wisdom in waiting for a divine answer.	**19** ♃♅℞▼ ⚷D ♓ 5:07 AM ☽ V/C 8:00 AM 10. Claim the now and enter the future.	**20** ♃♅℞▼ ☽ → ♋ 3:24 AM 2. At all times, be gentle with yourself.	**21** ♃♅℞ ☽ V/C 11:12 PM ☉ → ♐ 7:49 PM 3. Have fun being grateful.	**22** ♃♅℞ ☽ → ♌ 3:57 PM 4. Be loyal to yourself.	**23** ♃♅℞ 5. Procrastination delays progress.
24 ♃♅℞ ☽ V/C 1:00 AM 6. Your body is balancing differences and creating peace.	**25** ♃♅℞ ☽ → ♍ 4:12 AM 7. Being direct eliminates confusion.	**26** ♃♅℞ 8. Have courage in your convictions.	**27** ♃♅℞ ☽ V/C 3:45 AM ☽ → ♎ 2:01 PM 9. God is your essence which makes you divine.	**28** ♃♅℞ Thanksgiving Day Hanukkah 10. The wise person is innovative.	**29** ♃♅℞ ☽ V/C 3:14 AM ☽ → ♏ 8:04 PM 2. Keeping things in order is an advantage.	**30** ♃♅℞ 3. Be inspired by optimistic music.

November 2013 Planetary Highlights

Mercury is Retrograde in Scorpio until November 10

You may have to push the reset button frequently during this long sojourn for Mercury in Scorpio. Expect sarcasm and hard-edged, resentful remarks to be a part of life right now. Expect many communications that have been stored inside the deep well of the Scorpion shadow-self for years to be coming out. Watch out for the stinger!

November 6, 9:04 PM – Jupiter goes Retrograde in Cancer

Take time to recognize all of the blessings that have come home to you since 2001. The more you can find and recognize these blessings, the better your life will be. Jupiter is very happy in Cancer and good fortune will continue while he is there.

Neptune is Retrograde in Pisces until November 13

This will help us all emotionally to have Neptune going direct. The key here is not to feel so good that you put the rose-colored glasses back on.

Uranus Continues to be Retrograde in Aries all Month

The key here is to let instability do its work. Be spontaneous and learn to live in the power of the present rather than clinging to what you think you already know. When the ground is shaky, you are being presented with the gift of something new.

Chiron in Pisces stays Retrograde until November 19

Take time out to check your body to feel where healing is still needed. Then, do a scan on your thinking and look at what thoughts might still be damaging to your soul.

November 5, 12:44 AM – Venus enters Capricorn

All work and no play will frustrate Venus into a few brat attacks, especially with the holidays approaching. Try to keep the lid on the paint can and hold onto your hat! Duty-bound Capricorn will have her in his embrace until March 2014. Yikes! Best to learn how to be a practical princess.

November 3 – Highly Charged Field of Energy

The Moon, Sun, North Node, Mercury, and Saturn are all involved in a total solar eclipse in Scorpio. This is the last eclipse of the year and sets up a theme of accountability, practicality, and living from a realistic point of view. Create release from a 19-year pattern (1994).

November 15th Venus Snuggles up to Controlling Pluto

It is time to face our personal financial process. This could set in some challenges if you and your partner have different views on spending and saving.

November 21, 7:49 PM – The Sun enters Sagittarius

Party time—plan a trip and celebrate all the wonders in your world!

November 25 – Mercury meets up with Saturn again

It is a good idea to avoid using the word "should" to bypass conflict. At the same time, avoid reacting to the word "should" if it comes your way.

November 28 – Pluto-Uranus Square

A new ingredient is added when the Libra Moon enters the realm of the two rivals fighting for power. Diplomacy could save the day from the "off with your heads" process.

November 28 Venus and Jupiter Connect

This saves the day bringing joy, playfulness, and benefits to your Thanksgiving table. Jupiter's need for extravagance and indulgence may get carried away and have you needing to take some enzymes for digestion.

November 5-6 – Super-Sensitivity ▲

Pay attention to outside influences. The atmosphere is filled with negative thoughts, depression, and fear. Do your best to stay centered in your own process so you don't buy into the toxic global energy field.

November 20-21 – Low-Vitality ▼

Things are ending all around you during these days. Do your best to let them end and don't waste your energy holding on to what no longer has any life force. Your vitality is more important than anything. Do what it takes to be balanced.

♈ Aries	♋ Cancer	♐ Sagittarius	☽ Moon	♄ Saturn	☊ North Node	V/C	Void-of-Course
♉ Taurus	♌ Leo	♑ Capricorn	☿ Mercury	♅ Uranus	☋ South Node	▲	Super-Sensitivity
♊ Gemini	♍ Virgo	♒ Aquarius	♀ Venus	♆ Neptune	➡ Enters	▼	Low-Vitality
	♎ Libra	♓ Pisces	♂ Mars	♀ or ♇ Pluto	℞ Retrograde		
	♏ Scorpio	☉ Sun	♃ Jupiter	⚷ Chiron	S/D Stationary Direct		

New Moon in Scorpio

November 3, 4:51 AM – Solar Eclipse

Statement I Transform
Body Reproductive organs
Mind Investigation
Spirit Transformation

When the Sun is in Scorpio

Scorpio is the symbol of darkness which heralds the decline of the Sun in Autumn. Scorpio embodies the Law of Nature which decrees that even the strongest will must bow to the body's mortality. As we watch all of nature going through a slow death, we begin to recognize the qualities of Scorpio's subtlety and depth, and the hidden forces that threaten those who live only on the surface. Scorpio rules all of the things we try to keep hidden: death, taxes, power, money, sex, resentment, revenge, ambition, pride, and fear. When we face these self-imposed limits in ourselves, we take on the true power of transformation. Transformation establishes pathways for us to decentralize the ego in the interest of higher humanitarian work.

Scorpio Co-Creation Ideas

Now is the time to focus on...

- Transformation on all levels
- Bringing light to the dark
- Knowing and living cycles
- Knowing trust as an option
- Accepting change
- Accepting my sexuality
- Knowing sex is natural
- Knowing sex as good
- Knowing sex as creative

Scorpio Goddess

Persephone, the Goddess of the Underworld, is assigned to Scorpio. During the time of Scorpio, all of nature begins its sojourn into darkness in preparation for the void that comes in winter. Persephone is the harbinger of the Sun's decline. It is Persephone who asks us to release the idea of living on the surface in order to quest for the depth of our hidden forces, to recharge, rejuvenate, transform, and let go. Persephone rules our intuition, our inner beauty, the occult arts, and our ability to accept the cycles in nature that support our fertility, even when the cycle feels like death. Her domain comes alive in us every time we close our eyes. When the Moon is new in Scorpio, ask Persephone to guide you below the surface.

On Your Altar

Colors: Deep red, black, deep purple

Numerology: 3 – Celebrate your sensuality

Tarot Card: Death – the ability to transform, transmute, and transcend

Gemstones: Topaz, smoky quartz, obsidian, jet, onyx

Plant Remedy: Manzanita – being open to transforming cycles

Fragrance: Sandalwood – awakens your sensuality

New Moon in Scorpio

November 3, 4:51 AM – Solar Eclipse

Scorpio Challenges and Victories

"When the student needs to learn, the teacher appears." Today, I recognize that the Law of Reflection is in operation. I have become aware of this through my over-indulgence of judgment and criticism of other people. I am aware that when my judgment is running rampant, I am in need of a teacher who can interpret this judgment as reflection, so I can see my judgments as my teachers and use them to re-interpret myself. I seek counsel with someone who has the ability to listen to me, hear me, and give me the space I need to see myself. I have become confused by spending too much time looking outside myself for the answers. Perhaps my authority systems, like my religion or my family traditions, no longer serve me and I need to use this confusion to become aware of a new, more self-reliant way to live my life.

The Law of Reflection

Whatever I judge is what I am, what I fear, or what I lack. I make a list of my judgments:

I rewrite each judgment in the form of a question: Am I _____? Do I fear _____? Do I lack _____?

Example 1: I judge Mary's wealth. Do I fear wealth? Do I lack wealth? Am I wealthy in my own way and forgetting to acknowledge my own ability to manifest?

Example 2: I judge John's "be perfect" attitude. Do I fear perfection? Do I lack perfection? Have I forgotten to recognize my own perfection?

In moving through this process, I reconnect to myself and find my own authority today. I send blessings to others whose reflection has so beautifully shown me myself today. I now know and cherish my judgments as my greatest teachers and set myself free today.

Scorpio Homework

Scorpio co-creates best by being a private investigator, detective, in forensic medicine, probate attorney, mystery writer, mythologist, tarot reader, symbolist, hospice worker, transition counselor, mortician, and sex surrogate.

The Scorpio Moon cycle asks us to transform. In order to do this we must transmute sex drive into creativity, physical comfort into serving the greater good, money into higher value, fear into light, animosity into understanding, ambition into service to beauty, pride into humility, separation into unity, control into harmony, and power into empowerment.

New Moon in Scorpio

November 3, 4:51 AM – Solar Eclipse

Five Steps to Co-Creation

1. Acceptance

Acceptance opens the pathway to living in the moment and makes way for opportunity to occur. Co-creation can only occur when you live in the moment.

Start your list by writing… "I accept _____ into my life."

2. Adjustment

Consider what adjustments you may need to make in order to receive what you are accepting into your life.

My Co-Creation List

new Moon in Scorpio

November 3, 4:51 AM – Solar Eclipse

3. Awakening

Once your list is complete, use the power of sound and read your list out loud. This directs your intentions (your list) toward actualization and co-creation.

4. Alignment

Now it is time to make a petition to the Universe, using these words, "I call on the power of the Universe to know I am ready to receive my list. I accept it. I allow it. So be it! This, or something better than this, comes to me in an easy and pleasurable way for the good of all concerned. Thank You Universe!" Light your candle and place it on your eight-sided mirror.

5. Acknowledgement

When a creation result is acknowledged it seals the deal. This makes room for more magnificence to expand into your life and increases your abundance factor adding to your ability to receive.

As each aspect of your co-creation list arrives in your life, spend time allowing, acknowledging, and accepting it with the true gusto of gratitude. You might want to make a victory list here.

Victory List

Scorpio Questions to ask Myself

How can I share my money without being resentful?

What can I do to monitor my revenge and transform it into an expression of truth?

Where do I feel betrayed?

New Moon in Scorpio

November 3, 4:51 AM – Solar Eclipse

How to Use the Moon Book With Your Chart

Fill in the blanks on the Cosmic Check-In page. Then look up the degree of the moon on the chart below. Take note of the "I" statement on the outside of the wheel where the moon is located. Now locate the same degree on your own chart, and make a note of the house and corresponding "I" statement. Go back to the Cosmic Check-In page and circle the two statements from the charts and read what you wrote. This will give you an idea about what to expect from this moon phase on a personal level.

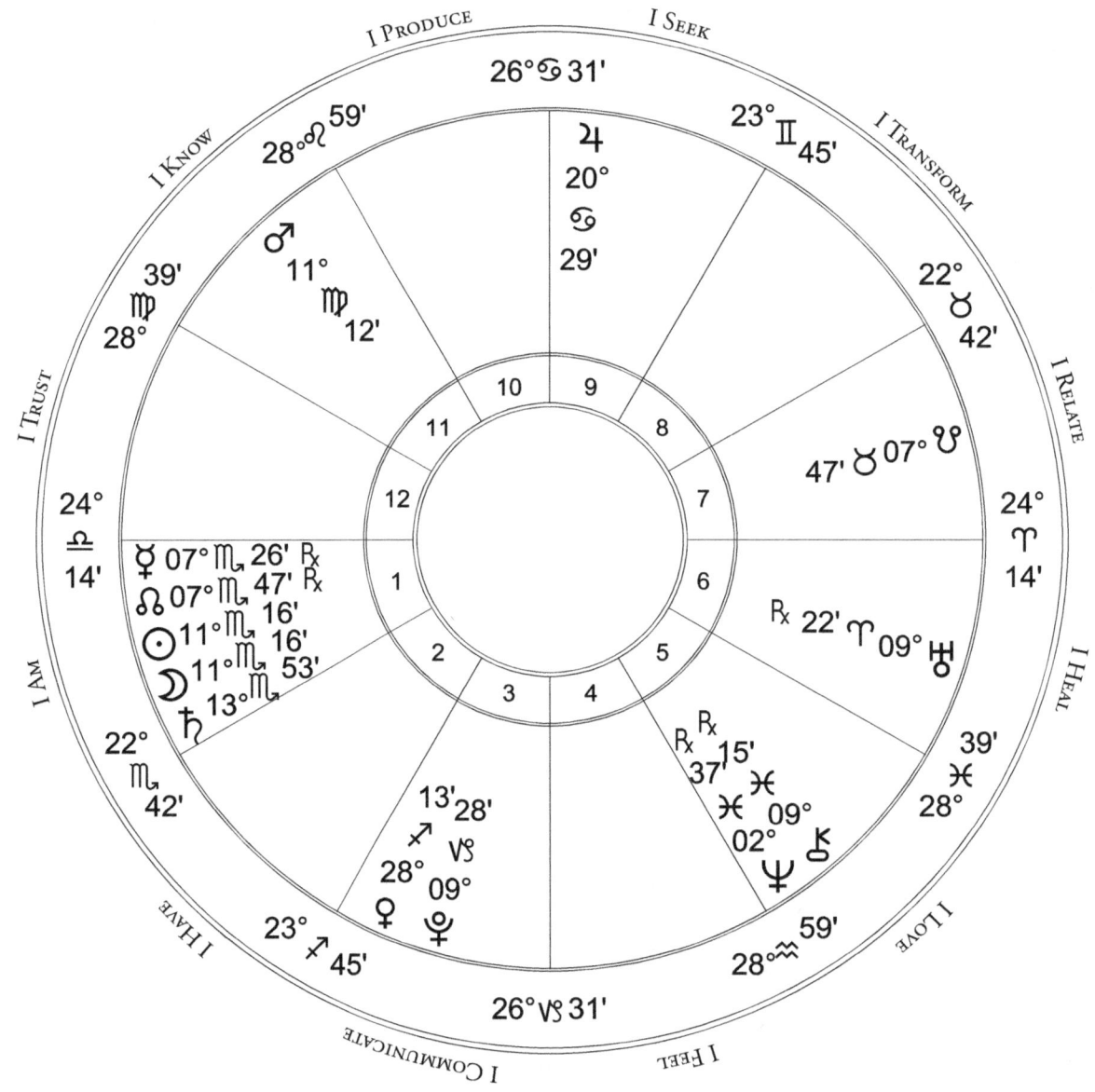

♈ Aries	♋ Cancer	♏ Scorpio	♓ Pisces	♀ Venus	♅ Uranus	☊ North Node
♉ Taurus	♌ Leo	♐ Sagittarius	☉ Sun	♂ Mars	♆ Neptune	☋ South Node
♊ Gemini	♍ Virgo	♑ Capricorn	☽ Moon	♃ Jupiter	♀ or ♇ Pluto	℞ Retrograde
	♎ Libra	♒ Aquarius	☿ Mercury	♄ Saturn	⚷ Chiron	

new Moon in Scorpio

November 3, 4:51 AM – Solar Eclipse

Cosmic Check-In

Take a moment to write a brief phrase for each "I" statement.
This activates all areas of your life for this creative cycle.

♏ I Transform

♐ I Seek

♑ I Produce

♒ I Know

♓ I Trust

♈ I Am

♉ I Have

♊ I Communicate

♋ I Feel

♌ I Love

♍ I Heal

♎ I Relate

Full Moon in Taurus

November 17, 7:17 AM

Statement I Have
Body Neck
Mind Collector
Spirit Accumulation

The Sun is Opposite the Moon

Full Moons are always in opposition to the Sun. This creates a feeling of tension between where you want to shine and how your feelings are flowing on a sensory level about the Sun's directive. The two forces seem like they are working against each other, yet they are on the same team displaying different techniques to attain the same goal. The Taurus/Scorpio polarity creates tension between shared resources and individual resources.

Taurus God

Ganesh is the Lord of Wisdom and Destroyer of All Obstacles. He grants success, prosperity, and protection against adversity. He is the deity that rules merchants and their trading. He rules Dharma by creating and removing obstacles appropriate to each individual's pathway. He is called the Lord of Wisdom because when we have earned the right to have an obstacle removed, we have learned the lesson and gained wisdom. Ganesh always appears with a rat at his feet. The rat is a symbol of desire, and desire always presents us with an obstacle to overcome in order to attain our wish. The rat shows up in secret places, stealing what does not belong to him. When the Moon is full in Taurus, it is time to put Ganesh into operation. Ask Ganesh to set us free from obstacles in order to gain wisdom and fulfill our desires.

Taurus Freedom List Ideas

Now is the time to free myself from…

- Envy
- Financial insecurity
- Being stubborn
- Hoarding
- Addictive spending
- Not feeling valuable
- Fear of change

On Your Altar

Colors: Scarlet, earth tones

Numerology: 6 – Let go of everything that doesn't feel beautiful

Tarot Card: Hierophant – spiritual authority

Gemstones: Red coral, red agate, garnet

Plant Remedy: Angelica – connecting Heaven and Earth

Fragrance: Rose – opening the heart

Full Moon in Taurus

November 17, 7:17 AM

Memory Maintenance Meditation

The Moon governs our memory and the maintenance of our memory. It is our memory that often creates blocks to setting us free to be able to attain our goals. The Moon works with us to help us become free from memory blocks three days after the Full Moon. The freedom themes are provided by the zodiac sign and can be from this lifetime or other lifetimes. These meditations assist in dissolving blocks and open pathways to new frontiers.

When the Moon is in Taurus, sit quietly, close your eyes, and breathe in and out. It is now time to search the Records of Stewardship to see where ownership of people and property may have been out of control. Look through the records to determine attitudes regarding possessions, objects of art, money, spending, lending, saving, and giving that may have been too extreme or impoverished. Ask for a Guardian Angel to show you where envy might be out of balance. Correct any dependency on others for their ability to acquire. Accept your own abundance factor.

Taurus Challenges and Victories

Everything is possible for me today. My possibilities are endless. I have the power within me to make all of my dreams come true. I have the tools to make my talent a reality. I have the power to identify with my talent. Today, I focus my attention and intention on manifesting with my talent and, in so doing, transform my ideas into reality. I recognize the part of me that is connected to the cosmic source of ideas and I express that source within me to manifest my creative power. I see my possibilities and act on them today. I am the creative power. I am all-knowing. I am an individual. There is no one else like me. I can manifest anything I desire. I intend it. I allow it. So be it.

Rules for Manifesting: know what you want, write it down, and say it out loud. Recognize that because you thought it, it can be so. Release your limiting beliefs. Override your limiting beliefs with power statements. Act as if you have already manifested your idea. Lastly, value yourself!

Taurus Homework

News flash for Taurus freedom process: consumerism is not practicing abundance. Take a look at what you have accumulated over the last few days, months, and years. Eliminate what no longer resonates to the beauty of the now. Take some of these items to a charity of your choice or give gifts to admiring friends. Take the Taurus freedom test and go to the store where you made your last purchase and return the items. Do not buy anything else. Remember, quality not quantity, and take the pledge to become a wise steward of your resources.

It's time to transform priorities from the external world of the centralized self, into the depth and subtlety of the hidden forces below the surface that connect us to the vastness of existence.

full Moon in Taurus

November 17, 7:17 AM

Five Steps to Freedom

When we work with the concept of freedom we are soon presented with resistance. Freedom presents a pathway for us to bump directly into our limitations. When we can become aware of these limits, we can then find our way to freedom. Below are some ideas that might assist you in seeing deeper into your resistance to accepting freedom into your life. Once you discover these you might want to add more to your freedom list.

1. Feeling Useless

This happens when you measure yourself by what others think of you.

2. Discouragement

This occurs when you use blame others instead of taking responsibility for your part in a situation.

3. Regret

This happens when you live inside past events and continue to rehearse your story, hoping that if you tell it enough, it will get resolved. Living in the past leads to regret and blocks you from freedom.

4. Limitation

This happens when we think that there is no way out of a challenge, which creates an inability to see options. When options are out of the picture we become unable to create positive outcomes.

5. Self-Doubt

This takes place when we think that others are better than we are. Growing cannot occur when we have given someone else our ceiling.

full Moon in Taurus

November 17, 7:17 AM

My Freedom List

Taurus Questions to Ask Myself

What makes me feel valuable?

What is the theme of my latest collection?

What must I do to take better care of my garden?

full Moon in Taurus

November 17, 7:17 AM

How to Use the Moon Book With Your Chart

Fill in the blanks on the Cosmic Check-In page. Then look up the degree of the moon on the chart below. Take note of the "I" statement on the outside of the wheel where the moon is located. Now locate the same degree on your own chart, and make a note of the house and corresponding "I" statement. Go back to the Cosmic Check-In page and circle the two statements from the charts and read what you wrote. This will give you an idea about what to expect from this moon phase on a personal level.

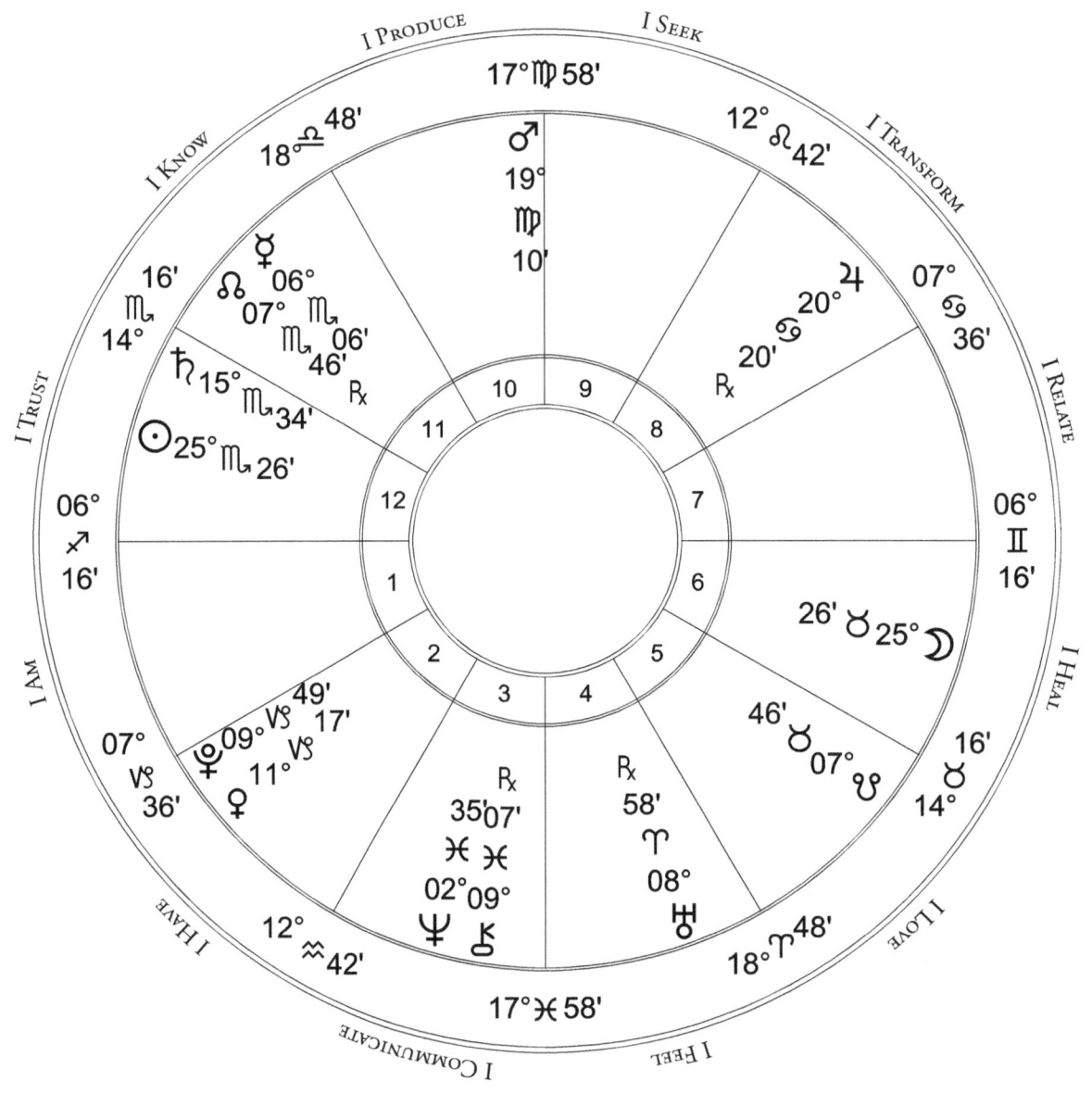

♈ Aries	♋ Cancer	♏ Scorpio	♓ Pisces	♀ Venus	♅ Uranus	☊ North Node
♉ Taurus	♌ Leo	♐ Sagittarius	☉ Sun	♂ Mars	♆ Neptune	☋ South Node
♊ Gemini	♍ Virgo	♑ Capricorn	☽ Moon	♃ Jupiter	♀ or ♇ Pluto	℞ Retrograde
♎ Libra		♒ Aquarius	☿ Mercury	♄ Saturn	⚷ Chiron	

full Moon in Taurus

November 17, 7:17 AM

Cosmic Check-In

Take a moment to write a brief phrase for each "I" statement.
This activates all areas of your life for this freedom cycle.

♉ I Have

♊ I Communicate

♋ I Feel

♌ I Love

♍ I Heal

♎ I Relate

♏ I Transform

♐ I Seek

♑ I Produce

♒ I Know

♓ I Trust

♈ I Am

December 2013

SUN	MON	TUE	WED	THU	FRI	SAT
1 ♃R ♂R ☽ V/C 5:35 PM ☽ → ♐ 10:32 PM 4. Being dogmatic lacks flexibility.	**2** ♃R ♂R ▲ ● 10°♐59' 4:23 PM 5. When we are understanding we are adaptable.	**3** ♃R ♂R ▲ ☽ V/C 7:46 PM ☽ → ♑ 10:50 PM 6. Surround yourself with beauty today.	**4** ♃R ♂R ☿ → ♐ 6:43 PM 7. Take time to look within.	**5** ♃R ♂R ☽ V/C 9:32 PM ☽ → ♒ 10:54 PM 8. Remember extravagance lacks balance.	**6** ♃R ♂R 9. Being alone is a spiritual impossibility.	**7** ♃R ♂R ☽ V/C 4:12 AM ♂ → ♎ 12:42 AM 10. You have the ability to change the past.
8 ♃R ♂R ☽ → ♓ 0:35 AM 2. Self-criticism lacks love.	**9** ♃R ♂R ☽ V/C 10:42 PM 3. Living in fear is an illusion.	**10** ♃R ♂R ☽ → ♈ 5:07 AM 4. Life is a transition.	**11** ♃R ♂R 5. Transmute rage into temperance.	**12** ♃R ♂R ☽ V/C 7:38 AM ☽ → ♉ 12:41 PM 6. Your growth requires being human.	**13** ♃R ♂R 7. Regardless of what you believe, the truth is the truth.	**14** ♃R ♂R ☽ V/C 6:55 PM ☽ → ♊ 10:41 PM 8. Reality is not static. It is always changing.
15 ♃R ♂R 9. Love is the most powerful force in the Universe.	**16** ♃R ♂R ▼ 10. Yesterday's directives need not apply today.	**17** ♃R ▼ ○ 25°♊36' 1:29 AM ☽ V/C 1:29 AM ♅R-8°♈35 9:40 AM ☽ → ♋ 10:18 AM 2. Take your time and stay in balance.	**18** ♃R 3. Smile at someone just for the fun of it.	**19** ♃R ☽ V/C 8:38 PM ☽ → ♌ 10:49 PM 4. Know the difference between economical and stingy.	**20** ♃R 5. Ride the wave of evolution.	**21** ♀R ♃R Winter Solstice ☉ → ♑ 9:12 AM ♀R-28°♑58' 1:54 PM 6. Love is the promise of the Universe.
22 ♀R ♃R ☽ V/C 5:2 AM ☽ → ♍ 11:20 AM 7. Remember your thoughts are energy.	**23** ♀R ♃R 8. Trust the abundance factor to work in your favor.	**24** ♀R ♃R ☿ → ♑ 2:13 AM ☽ V/C 7:56 PM ☽ → ♎ 10:18 PM 9. Miracles are the result of your own divine process.	**25** ♀R ♃R Christmas Day 10. Have a joyous celebration.	**26** ♀R ♃R Kwanzaa 2. Double your love today.	**27** ♀R ♃R ☽ V/C 3:01 AM ☽ → ♏ 5:59 AM 3. Imagine it and create it.	**28** ♀R ♃R 4. Patience creates stability today.
29 ♀R ♃R ☽ V/C 5:55 AM ☽ → ♐ 9:38 AM 5. Being inconsistent is different than change.	**30** ♀R ♃R ▲ ☽ V/C 3:37 AM 6. Feel the beauty and grace that surrounds you.	**31** ♀R ♃R ▲ New Year's Eve ☽ → ♑ 10:02 AM 7. Be grateful for the past year.				

210

December 2013 Planetary Highlights

Jupiter Retrograde in Cancer all Month

Expect an old love to show up for the holidays. We will be reviewing love, home, and family life left over from 2001. Whatever you left back there will show up to be reviewed. Allow yourself to make new choices and move on.

Uranus Retrograde in Aries until December 17

We are asked to be complete on all of our unfinished projects so that we can be free to move forward to new areas of endeavor with true enthusiasm. Do what it takes to cross the finish line so the true spirit of Uranus' inner freedom theme can be yours. Celebrate your completion with a ritual so your cellular structure will be able to open to receive your new magnetic matrix for your future. Prepare to become your future self !!!

December 21, 1:54 PM – Venus Retrograde in Capricorn

This is a reality check on relationship. The challenge here is romance versus responsibility which can create tension and frustration on either end of the spectrum. Expect to feel rejection, insecurity, possessiveness, and invalidation of the present by clinging to the past during this transit. The best way to work with this pattern is to practice the art of knowing "when to hold them and knowing when to fold them." Remember, Venus' needs are always urgent and Capricorn needs to be practical; discern the appropriate plan for action through careful thought.

December 4, 6:43 PM – Mercury enters Sagittarius

Mercury is so happy to be out of the misery of Scorpio's hidden world and is moving into the Sagittarius realm of optimism. The carefree attitude can get you in trouble if you fall into the exaggerative process and take a risk that will be regretted later. The rule of thumb here is to say what you mean and mean what you say.

December 21, 9:12 AM – Winter Solstice – The Sun enters Capricorn

Celebrate the solstice with a special event, such as a ceremony of lights. Today is the darkest day of the year and marks the point when the new light begins to last a bit longer each day. This light is the light of new awareness to be developed in the consciousness of mankind for the coming year. It is the Earth's birthday—celebrate and honor her today!

December 2 and 3, 30 and 31 – Super-Sensitivity ▲

Depression can take over and drag you down to the deepest part of your inner self if you let it take over. Pay attention and don't "numb out" to escape your feelings. Addictions are in great demand this month due to the illusions that are running rampant in the atmosphere.

December 16 and 17 – Low-Vitality ▼

Let go and know that everything is changing around you. When things come to their end, don't push to keep them alive. Celebrate the ending and know that the Law of Balance will honor the empty space by bringing you something new.

♈ Aries	♋ Cancer	♐ Sagittarius	☽ Moon	♄ Saturn	☊ North Node	V/C Void-of-Course
♉ Taurus	♌ Leo	♑ Capricorn	☿ Mercury	♅ Uranus	☋ South Node	▲ Super-Sensitivity
♊ Gemini	♍ Virgo	♒ Aquarius	♀ Venus	♆ Neptune	➡ Enters	▼ Low-Vitality
	♎ Libra	♓ Picses	♂ Mars	♀ or ♇ Pluto	℞ Retrograde	
	♏ Scorpio	☉ Sun	♃ Jupiter	⚷ Chiron	S/D Stationary Direct	

New Moon in Sagittarius

December 2, 4:23 PM

Statement I Seek
Body Thighs
Mind Philosophical
Spirit Inspiration

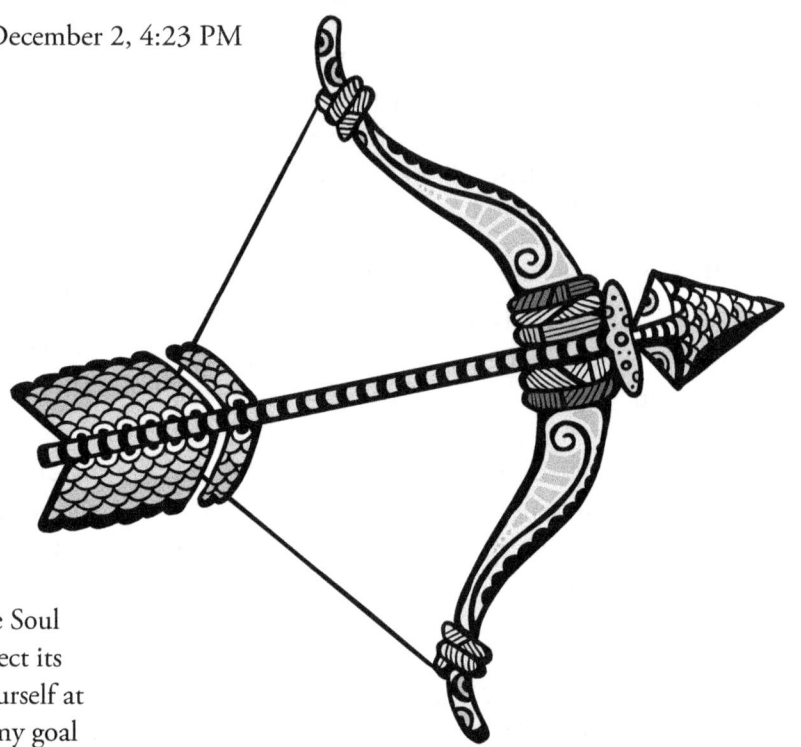

When the Sun is in Sagittarius

Now is the time for greater expansion of consciousness. Sagittarius is about exterminating all of the man-eating symbols of our illusions, harmful thoughts, inertia, prejudices, and superstitions that hide behind our excuses. It is truth time, so that the Soul Goal of the Sagittarius can come into being and direct its light toward greater aspiration. Questions to ask yourself at this time are: What is my goal for myself? What is my goal for my nation? What is my goal for humanity? All goals get stimulated during this time.

Sagittarius Goddess

The Sagittarius goddess, Saraswati, is in charge of fusing our personality with the light of our inner divinity. When this fusion occurs, the Law of Sound is made available to us and we have the power to manifest by directing our vision through the resonance of our own tone, note, or voice. The power of speech reaches a high level with Saraswati, the Goddess of Speech and Knowledge. The activation of sound sheds light on our path, directing us toward the magnetic matrix of our future, our goals. Saraswati reminds us that everything we put to sound ultimately manifests. It is in our best interest to avoid harmful speech, gossip, and our story, in order to be present with the power of the moment. Call on Saraswati to deliver you to your point of experience that provides the knowledge you are here to gain.

Sagittarius Co-Creation Ideas

Now is the time to focus on...

- Truth
- Teaching and study
- Understanding advanced ideas
- Optimism and inspiration
- Bliss
- Goals
- Travel and adventure
- Philosophy and culture

On Your Altar

Colors: Deep purple, deep blue, turquoise

Numerology: 6 – Pay attention to what you love

Tarot Card: Temperance – blending physical and spiritual

Gemstones: Turquoise, lapis

Plant Remedy: Madia – seeing the target and hitting it

Fragrance: Magnolia – expanded beauty

new Moon in Sagittarius

December 2, 4:23 PM

Sagittarius Challenges and Victories

Destiny is in my favor today. I know without a doubt that I cannot make a wrong turn today. I access my blueprint to ensure perfect timing for all opportunities to be open to me today. I promise to be open to these opportunities knowing full well that today is my day. I am on time and in time today. My destiny is here and working in my favor. I see all that is available to me today and claim my pathway to success. I pay attention to what comes my way today and know that it is an opening for good fortune to be my reality. I am ready to accept my good fortune now. All I have to do is move in the direction of my truth. I know that my truth is my good fortune. I trust in coincidence and synchronicity to provide me with direction to my destiny. All points of action lead me to my true expression. I can see clearly into my future today with great optimism. I intend it. I allow it. So be it. All is in Divine Order.

Mantra during this Time *(repeat this 10 times out loud)*

"My truth is my good fortune. My timing is perfect. I trust that all that comes to me today is in my highest and best good. I am open to optimism. The drum of destiny beats in my favor. So be it!"

Sagittarius Homework

Sagittarius co-creates best through teaching, publishing and writing, travel, spiritual adventures, and as tour group leaders, airline and cruise ship personnel, evangelical ministers, philosophers, anthropologists, linguists, and translators.

The Sagittarius moon cycle creates a magnetic matrix that stimulates us to take direction towards becoming one with a goal and then sheds light on the path. In the ancient mystery schools, Sagittarius moons were used to set the stage for candidates to reach higher levels of awareness by inspiring their desire to reach a goal and then to step toward the goal. It is time now to become one with my goal.

New Moon in Sagittarius

December 2, 4:23 PM

Five Steps to Co-Creation

1. Acceptance

Acceptance opens the pathway to living in the moment and makes way for opportunity to occur. Co-creation can only occur when you live in the moment.

Start your list by writing... "I accept _____ into my life."

2. Adjustment

Consider what adjustments you may need to make in order to receive what you are accepting into your life.

My Co-Creation List

new Moon in Sagittarius

December 2, 4:23 PM

3. Awakening

Once your list is complete, use the power of sound and read your list out loud. This directs your intentions (your list) toward actualization and co-creation.

4. Alignment

Now it is time to make a petition to the Universe, using these words, "I call on the power of the Universe to know I am ready to receive my list. I accept it. I allow it. So be it! This, or something better than this, comes to me in an easy and pleasurable way for the good of all concerned. Thank You Universe!" Light your candle and place it on your eight-sided mirror.

5. Acknowledgement

When a creation result is acknowledged it seals the deal. This makes room for more magnificence to expand into your life and increases your abundance factor adding to your ability to receive.

As each aspect of your co-creation list arrives in your life, spend time allowing, acknowledging, and accepting it with the true gusto of gratitude. You might want to make a victory list here.

Victory List

Sagittarius Questions to ask Myself

Where have I placed the illusion of glamour in front of my truth?

Where can I align my purpose to make the best use of myself?

In this moment can I set the stage for my soul goal to become fully alive in my presence?

new Moon in Sagittarius

December 2, 4:23 PM

How to Use the Moon Book With Your Chart

Fill in the blanks on the Cosmic Check-In page. Then look up the degree of the moon on the chart below. Take note of the "I" statement on the outside of the wheel where the moon is located. Now locate the same degree on your own chart, and make a note of the house and corresponding "I" statement. Go back to the Cosmic Check-In page and circle the two statements from the charts and read what you wrote. This will give you an idea about what to expect from this moon phase on a personal level.

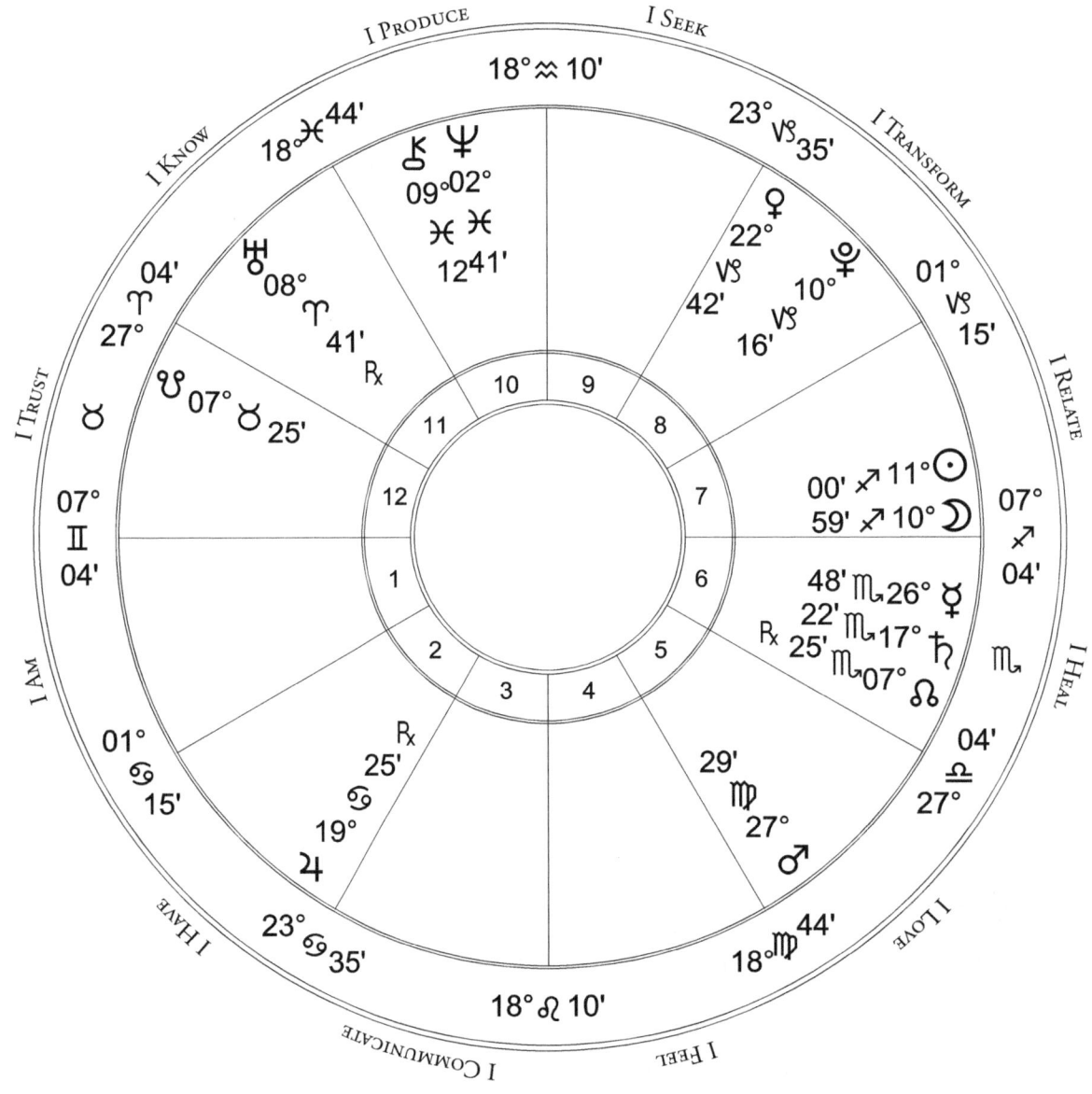

♈ Aries	♋ Cancer	♏ Scorpio	♓ Pisces	♀ Venus	♅ Uranus	☊ North Node
♉ Taurus	♌ Leo	♐ Sagittarius	☉ Sun	♂ Mars	♆ Neptune	☋ South Node
♊ Gemini	♍ Virgo	♑ Capricorn	☽ Moon	♀ or ♇ Pluto	⚷ Chiron	℞ Retrograde
	♎ Libra	♒ Aquarius	☿ Mercury	♃ Jupiter	♄ Saturn	

new Moon in Sagittarius

December 2, 4:23 PM

Cosmic Check-In

Take a moment to write a brief phrase for each "I" statement.
This activates all areas of your life for this creative cycle.

♐ I Seek

♑ I Produce

♒ I Know

♓ I Trust

♈ I Am

♉ I Have

♊ I Communicate

♋ I Feel

♌ I Love

♍ I Heal

♎ I Relate

♏ I Transform

Full Moon in Gemini

December 17, 1:29 AM

Statement I Communicate
Body Lungs
Mind Duplicity
Spirit Communication

The Sun is Opposite the Moon

Full Moons are always in opposition to the Sun. This creates a feeling of tension between where you want to shine and how your feelings are flowing on a sensory level about the Sun's directive. The two forces seem like they are working against each other, yet they are on the same team displaying different techniques to attain the same goal. The Gemini/Sagittarius polarity creates tension between community ideas and global thinking.

Gemini Goddess

Echo means, "one who loves her own voice." Echo was a very talkative nymph in the garden of Bacchus. Zeus visited this garden often to survey the desirable nymphs. He was enchanted by the gregarious Echo and began his conquest for her. Hera, Zeus' wife, showed up just as Zeus was about to consummate his passion for Echo. Hera was so jealous that she punished the talkative Echo for flirting with her husband. She took away Echo's ability to converse, leaving her to repeat the last three words of other people's sentences. When the Moon is full in Gemini, it is time to look at our mindless chatter and release repeating thoughts that echo in the chamber of our mind.

Gemini Freedom List Ideas

Now is the time to free myself from…

- Unfinished business
- Shallow communication
- Old files and office clutter
- Lies I tell myself
- Broken communication devices
- Temptation to gossip
- Restlessness and over-thinking
- Vacillation

On Your Altar

Colors: Bright Yellow, orange, multi-colors

Numerology: 9 – Stay connected to Spirit

Tarot Card: Lovers – connecting to wholeness

Gemstones: Yellow diamond, citrine, yellow jade, yellow topaz

Plant Remedy: Morning Glory – thinking with your heart, not your head

Fragrance: Iris – the ability to focus the mind

Full Moon in Gemini

December 17, 1:29 AM

Memory Maintenance Meditation

The Moon governs our memory and the maintenance of our memory. It is our memory that often creates blocks to setting us free to be able to attain our goals. The Moon works with us to help us become free from memory blocks three days after the Full Moon. The freedom themes are provided by the zodiac sign and can be from this lifetime or other lifetimes. These meditations assist in dissolving blocks and open pathways to new frontiers.

When the Moon is in Gemini, it is a time to review the split between your spiritual nature and your worldly nature. Sit down and close your eyes. Breathe in and breathe out. Ask for the Angel of Blending to bring you awareness of your double-mindedness, double-speaking, criticism of others, discontent, and mental unrest. Become aware of separation issues that divide you from your personal truth. Become a unifier rather than a divider.

Gemini Challenges and Victories

Today I blend my old self with my new self, my physical reality with my spiritual awareness, my positive thoughts with my negative thoughts, my past with my present, my feminine with my masculine, my rewards with my losses, my ups with my downs, and my higher self with my lower self. It is a day for me to refine and fine tune my life by looking at my extremes. I recognize what inspires me and what keeps me stuck. I find my center today by acknowledging my extremes. I am aware that balance comes to those who are able to locate the space in the center of these opposite energy fields.

When I am in my center, my polarities are in motion. Healing cannot occur unless my polarities are moving and I know that healing is motion. I am ready for a healing today and know that by visiting my opposites, and determining their vast opposition to each other, I can find the paradoxes that I have chosen for myself and begin to heal. I am willing to experiment with this blending of opposites and become the alchemist of my own life. When I blend all aspects of myself rather than separating them, I can truly become whole. Today is a day to integrate rather than separate in order to release the spark of light that stays a prisoner when my polarities are in operation. When I find balance, motion occurs and the Law of Harmony takes over, putting paradoxical energies to rest, thus breaking the crystallization of polarity. The Law of Harmony is beauty in motion, promoting the flow of color, light, sound, and movement into form. Balance is a condition that keeps my spark in motion. I become the vertical line in the center of polarity today and carry the secret of balance. Balance cannot be my goal, motion is my goal today. When I am in motion I can take action to evolve and to express all of myself freely.

Gemini Homework

Sit still, and invite silence into your space. Stay quiet and still for at least 5 minutes. During this time take an inventory and see where you have interrupted people in the middle of their sentences. Now is the time to make a conscious effort to allow others the space to express their thoughts. Keep sitting there in silence and feel the frustration, while embracing the power of silence.

Full Moon in Gemini

December 17, 1:29 AM

Five Steps to Freedom

When we work with the concept of freedom we are soon presented with resistance. Freedom presents a pathway for us to bump directly into our limitations. When we can become aware of these limits, we can then find our way to freedom. Below are some ideas that might assist you in seeing deeper into your resistance to accepting freedom into your life. Once you discover these you might want to add more to your freedom list.

1. Feeling Useless

This happens when you measure yourself by what others think of you.

2. Discouragement

This occurs when you use blame others instead of taking responsibility for your part in a situation.

3. Regret

This happens when you live inside past events and continue to rehearse your story, hoping that if you tell it enough, it will get resolved. Living in the past leads to regret and blocks you from freedom.

4. Limitation

This happens when we think that there is no way out of a challenge, which creates an inability to see options. When options are out of the picture we become unable to create positive outcomes.

5. Self-Doubt

This takes place when we think that others are better than we are. Growing cannot occur when we have given someone else our ceiling.

full Moon in Gemini

December 17, 1:29 AM

My Freedom List

Gemini Questions to Ask Myself

What excuses do I use to keep putting things off?

Where am I still stuck in the idea that I have to be right?

Where am I still vacillating?

full Moon in Gemini

December 17, 1:29 AM

How to Use the Moon Book With Your Chart

Fill in the blanks on the Cosmic Check-In page. Then look up the degree of the moon on the chart below. Take note of the "I" statement on the outside of the wheel where the moon is located. Now locate the same degree on your own chart, and make a note of the house and corresponding "I" statement. Go back to the Cosmic Check-In page and circle the two statements from the charts and read what you wrote. This will give you an idea about what to expect from this moon phase on a personal level.

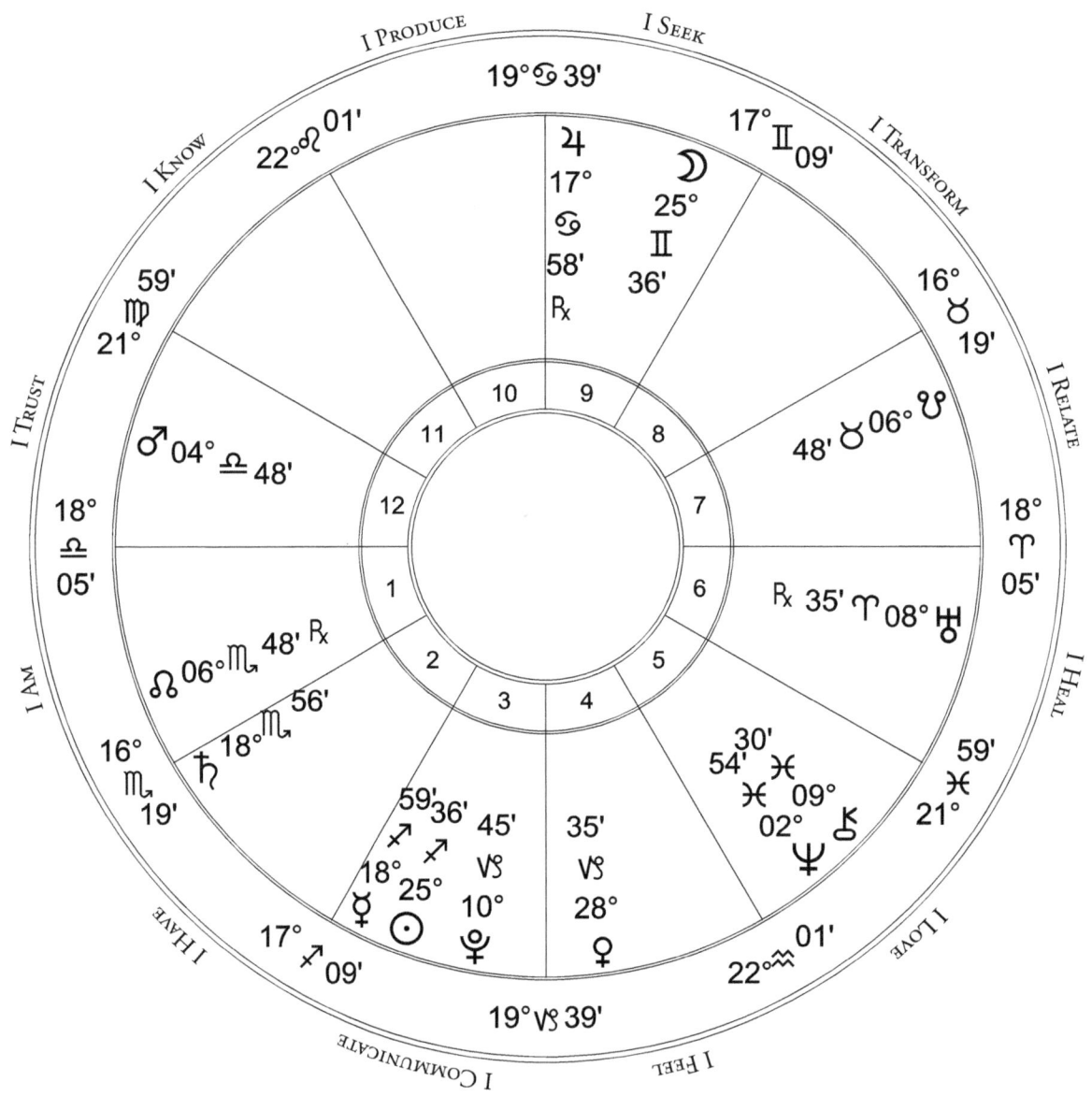

♈ Aries	♋ Cancer	♏ Scorpio	♓ Pisces	♀ Venus	♅ Uranus	☊ North Node
♉ Taurus	♌ Leo	♐ Sagittarius	☉ Sun	♂ Mars	♆ Neptune	☋ South Node
♊ Gemini	♍ Virgo	♑ Capricorn	☽ Moon	♃ Jupiter	♀ or ♇ Pluto	℞ Retrograde
	♎ Libra	♒ Aquarius	☿ Mercury	♄ Saturn	⚷ Chiron	

224

full Moon in Gemini

December 17, 1:29 AM

Cosmic Check-In

Take a moment to write a brief phrase for each "I" statement.
This activates all areas of your life for this freedom cycle.

♊ I Communicate

♋ I Feel

♌ I Love

♍ I Heal

♎ I Relate

♏ I Transform

♐ I Seek

♑ I Produce

♒ I Know

♓ I Trust

♈ I Am

♉ I Have

about The Author

Beatrex Quntanna

is a dynamic teacher devoted to the growth and development of the human potential. She inspires, motivates, and stimulates growth with her ever-present zest for life and the human experience. Beatrex is an author, lecturer, symbolist and Tarot expert. She has been counseling and teaching for the past thirty years using the Tarot as an enhancement for personal and intuitive development. Her students find her workshops and books inspiring, enlightening, full of wise truths, and helpful in pursuing the most positive outcome in their own lives.

Other books written by Beatrex are:
Tarot: A Universal Language.

Interested in personal readings with Beatrex, and ongoing Moon Classes and workshops? Contact her at beatrex@cox.net or visit her at www.beatrex.com

For Moon-related products created by Beatrex go to www.IamLivingByTheLightOfTheMoon.com

Tarot
A Universal Language

By Beatrex Quntanna

**Experiencing The Road of Life
Through the Magic of Symbols**

The symbology of each Major and Minor card are an awakening to the inner-wisdom of the Tarot—each card comes alive to a new light with upbeat, positive definitions that reflect Beatrex' fresh approach to life and living, making self-discovery easy and fun!

- Easy to use and easy to understand

- Includes an interpretation of all 78 Tarot cards right-side-up and reversed, in full-color

- Filled with innovative and informative readings for the reader to dive deep into the pool of knowledge and discover how to live vibrantly

Enthusiastic readers call it,

"Brilliantly Engineered"
"Amazingly Accurate"
"A refreshing, uncluttered approach to learning the Tarot."

To order, call 1-760-944-6020
or go to www.Beatrex.com

www.ingramcontent.com/pod-product-compliance
Lightning Source LLC
Chambersburg PA
CBHW080730230426
43665CB00020B/2690